Reading
PLAN

Dear Student,

Welcome to American Book Company's PLAN series! This series has been made just for you! Every book will give you practice for 100 percent of the PLAN standards. Our writers covered each standard as clearly and simply as possible.

Our writers have also included Depth of Knowledge (DOK) levels in these books. You will see the levels in the chapters and the practice questions. These leveled questions will increase your ability to understand new concepts.

Also, with each PLAN book, we have included free online testing from now until August 2014. If you have one of these books, the link and code are listed at the bottom of this page.

Using the code, go online and take the Post Test. Use this tool to find out which skills you already know. You can also discover which skills will need more work. When you finish the test, print out the results. Then give them to your teacher.

After you are done, you can use the book in different ways. You can work through all of the material in the book, paying close attention to the areas where you made mistakes. Or, if you do not have much time, you can only work on the parts where you made the most mistakes. Two additional full length tests, one at the front, the other at the end, are available within the book for skills mastery.

We look forward to hearing of your success when you see your PLAN results!

Sincerely,

Frank J Pintozzi

Dr. Frank Pintozzi
Executive Vice President
American Book Company
www.americanbookcompany.com
888-264-5877

Scan this QR code with your smart device to jump to the online testing page.

To access your pretest and post test, **visit americanbookcompany.com/online-testing/test.php** and select **"PLAN Reading Post Test."** Enter the password **"story"** to access these tests.

American Book Company
The Standards Experts

PLAN® READING TEST PREPARATION GUIDE

2013-2014 Edition

Author: Kindred Howard

Project Coordinator: Zuzana Urbanek

American Book Company
PO Box 2638
Woodstock, GA 30188-1383
Toll Free: 1 (888) 264-5877   Phone: (770) 928-2834
Toll Free Fax: 1 (866) 827-3240
website: www.americanbookcompany.com

ACKNOWLEDGEMENTS

The authors would like to gratefully acknowledge the technical contributions of Marsha Torrens and Becky Wright, the editing contribution of Mallory Grantham, and the proofreading expertise of Susan Barrows and Brittany Rowland.

We also want to thank Mary Stoddard for her expertise in developing many of the graphics for this book.

© 2013 American Book Company
PO Box 2638
Woodstock, GA 30188-1318

ALL RIGHTS RESERVED

The text of this publication, or any part thereof, may not be reproduced or transmitted in any form or by any means, electronic or mechanical, including photocopying, recording, storage in an information retrieval system, or otherwise, without the prior written permission of the publisher.

Printed in the United States of America

05/13

Table of Contents

Preface	iii
Diagnostic Test	**1**
Diagnostic Test Evaluation Chart	11
Chapter 1: What to Expect and How to Prepare	**13**
What to Expect on the PLAN Reading Test	13
Test Content	13
Types of Questions	14
Diagnostic and Practice Tests	14
Frequently Asked Questions	15
Tips for PLAN Preparation and Testing	15
Preparing for the PLAN	16
Taking the PLAN	16
How the PLAN Reading Test Will Look	18
Sample Passage with Explanations	19
Reading Forward	24
Chapter 2: Understanding the Main Idea, Supporting Details, and Author's Approach	**25**
Main Idea	26
Directly Stated Main Idea	26
Implied Main Idea	28
Supporting Details	31
Basic Facts	31
Events and Examples	32
Supporting Details and Implied Main Ideas	32
Interpreting Details	32
Recognizing Details That Support a Specific Point	33
Recognizing the Function of a Part of a Passage	37
Author's Approach	40
Author's Clear Intent	41
Chapter 2 Summary	44
Chapter 2 Review	45

Table of Contents

Chapter 3: Reading for Relationships: Sequential Order, Connections, and Cause-Effect — 51

Sequential Order 52
Relationships between People, Characters, Ideas, and Events 55
    Comparison and Contrast 55
    Cause-Effect Relationships 56
Chapter 3 Summary 60
Chapter 3 Review 61

Chapter 4: Interpreting Words and Phrases — 65

Understanding Words and Phrases 65
    Descriptive Language 66
    Figurative Language 67
Understanding Context 72
Chapter 4 Summary 78
Chapter 4 Review 78

Chapter 5: Generalizations and Conclusions — 81

Drawing Generalizations 81
Drawing Conclusions 87
Chapter 5 Summary 95
Chapter 5 Review 96

Practice Test — 101

Index — 111

Preface

The *PLAN® Reading Test Preparation Guide* will help students preparing to take the PLAN Reading Test. The most up-to-date requirements and strategies for the PLAN Reading Test are covered in this book. PLAN® is a registered trademark of ACT series, Inc. American Book Company is not affiliated with ACT, Inc., and produced this book independently.

This book contains several sections: 1) general information about the book, 2) a complete diagnostic reading test, 3) an evaluation chart, 4) chapters that review the strategies, concepts, and skills that improve readiness for the PLAN Reading Test, and 5) a complete practice reading test. Answers to the practice test, chapter practices, and chapter reviews are in a separate manual.

We welcome comments and suggestions about the book. Please contact the authors at

American Book Company
PO Box 2638
Woodstock, GA 30188-1383

Toll Free: 1 (888) 264-5877
Phone: (770) 928-2834
Fax: (770) 928-7483
Website: www.americanbookcompany.com

Preface

About the Author:

Kindred Howard is a 1991 alumnus of the University of North Carolina at Chapel Hill, where he graduated with a B.S. in criminal justice and national honors in political science. In addition to two years as a probation and parole officer in North Carolina, he has served for over twelve years as a teacher and writer in the fields of religion and social studies. His experience includes teaching students at both the college and high school level, as well as speaking at numerous seminars and authoring several books on US history, American government, geography, and economics. Mr. Howard is currently completing an M.A. in history from Georgia State University. Mr. Howard lives in Powder Springs, Georgia, with his wife and five children.

About the Project Coordinator:

Zuzana Urbanek serves as ELA Curriculum Coordinator for American Book Company. She is a professional writer and editor with over twenty-five years of experience in education, business, and publishing. She has taught a variety of English courses at the college level and also has taught English as a foreign language abroad. Her master's degree is from Arizona State University.

PLAN Reading Test
Diagnostic Test

20 minutes — 25 questions

Directions: There are three passages in this test. Read each of the passages, and then answer the questions that follow. Choose the best answer to each question based on your reading of the passage. You may refer to the passage as often as needed.

Passage I

Directions: Read the passage below. Then answer the questions that follow it. Choose the best answer to each question based on your reading of the passage. You may refer to the passage as often as needed.

PROSE FICTION: This passage is adapted from Elizabeth Sutherland's "The Gravel Road" (©2010 Rameses Publishing).

Mountain mornings are chilly in western North Carolina, even in the early fall. Sometimes there's even a touch of frost. There was on this
5   particular morning. I can still remember being a little cold and able to see my own breath as I headed down the old gravel road my brother, sister, and I had traversed so many times before. Like
10 most Saturdays, the three of us rose early, grabbed our rusty metal buckets, and headed off to pick blackberries. Picking blackberries was how we earned money to buy school supplies.
15 I'm not sure how far we actually walked most weeks to reach our prime blackberry-picking spot. I just remember that the walk always seemed too long and too short at the same time.
20 It seemed long because we walked and walked, until the shabby, blue-collar trailer park where we lived was no longer visible and had given way to nothing but woods and the sound of
25 gravel beneath our feet. The walk back seemed even longer. By the time we'd finished picking blackberries we were tired, and the early morning chill had long since given way to the exhausting
30 heat of the early afternoon sun.

And, yet, the walk never seemed long enough. The walk along that gravel road and the time spent in the blackberry field was, if nothing
35 else, an escape. It was the closest to freedom my siblings and I knew. It was the one time each week we were together without the feeling that we might be beaten, verbally abused, or
40 humiliated as the butt of some other kid's cruel comment or a teacher's insensitive remark. Along that quiet gravel road and in that open field, it was just us. There we weren't abandoned,
45 orphaned kids. We were just brother and sisters. We didn't have to worry about what the world thought of us—at least for a few hours. We could just be together. We could just be, period.

50 But this day's trek down the gravel road was different. This time, I walked with nervous anticipation. I wasn't sure if I should be scared or excited … worried or hopeful. My brother and
55 sister suspected nothing; to them, it was just another Saturday's hike to pick blackberries. As we walked along, the sound of rocks and dirt shuffling under our worn, dragging shoes, the sun
60 gradually broke through the surrounding trees. My baby sister and older brother occasionally made small talk or stopped to pick up a random stick. I can't remember anything they
65 said, I just remember that they seemed normal, the same way they always did. Perhaps they noticed I was quieter than usual—distracted. If they did, they didn't say anything. They didn't seem to
70 notice anything was wrong or different. But even if they had, there's a good chance they still wouldn't have

mentioned it. Our blackberry expeditions constituted the one time a week we chose to leave the despair of our daily existence behind, if only for a little while, in that dingy, foul-smelling trailer we called home. We dealt with enough sadness and anxiety every other moment of our lives; more than any kids our age ever should. The last thing any of us wanted to do was to disrupt our blackberry-picking expedition with any talk of concerns or dread. It's understandable if they chose to ignore any vibe of worry I might have been giving off that morning. Why risk weighing down our few moments of weekly freedom with talk and thoughts of the hell we lived in day to day?

1. From the passage, the reader can infer which of the following?

   A. People who live in the mountains pick blackberries once a week.
   B. Time spent together is the closest thing to freedom many kids know.
   C. You can often see your own breath in the air on chilly mornings.
   D. Mountain children commonly pick blackberries to buy school supplies.

2. The passage suggests that the narrator values the walks along the gravel road as something that:
   F. affords her an escape from reality.
   G. enables her to earn money.
   H. allows her time to think.
   J. reminds her of her peaceful home.

3. It is clear from the passage that the narrator and her siblings:
   A. are not very close.
   B. have a happy home life.
   C. are popular in school.
   D. don't live with their parents.

4. The statement in lines 54–57 that reads "My brother and sister suspected nothing; to them, it was just another Saturday's hike to pick blackberries" implies that:
   F. the narrator is plotting against her brother and sister.
   G. the narrator knows something her brother and sister don't.
   H. the narrator has no intention of going back home.
   J. the brother and sister are not as smart as the narrator.

5. The home life of the three children best can be described as:
   A. happy.
   B. gifted.
   C. exciting.
   D. difficult.

6. In lines 21–22, what does the phrase "shabby, blue-collar trailer park" suggest about the children?
   F. They live in an orphanage.
   G. They live in a poor environment.
   H. They live in a rich neighborhood.
   J. They live in an abusive home.

Diagnostic Test

7. According to the passage, how is the narrator's demeanor different from normal on this expedition?

    A. She is happier than most days.

    B. She is more talkative than normal.

    C. She is more nervous than usual.

    D. She is angrier than she usually is.

8. To get to the blackberry field, the narrator and her siblings have to:

    F. walk for miles along a river.

    G. trek through the woods.

    H. travel around a trailer park.

    J. sneak past mean kids from school.

Passage II

Directions: Read the passage below. Then answer the questions that follow it. Choose the best answer to each question based on your reading of the passage. You may refer to the passage as often as needed.

SOCIAL SCIENCES: This passage is adapted from the high school social studies book *Passing the Oklahoma End-of-Course Test in US History* by Kindred Howard (©2009 American Book Company).

Historians are people who study the past for a living. Historians rely on documentary sources to help them understand past periods and events. The
5 two types of documentary sources that historians rely on are primary sources and secondary sources. Primary sources are writings, documents, pictures, oral accounts, and so on that come from the
10 specific time a historian is studying. If a historian is studying World War II, then letters written by soldiers during that war, newspapers printed at the time of the war, photographs taken during the
15 war, and oral interviews with people who had fought in the war would all be primary sources. Secondary sources consist of information that comes from other researchers who have already
20 studied primary sources to create their own works about the subject. When a student reads online articles, encyclopedias, or historical books, or watches a documentary about a past
25 event, he or she is learning from secondary sources.

When studying documentary sources, it is very important that historians distinguish between fact and
30 opinion. Facts tell a historian what has happened in the past. Opinions simply give a narrow interpretation of what has happened in the past. Facts cannot be disputed: The American colonists
35 defeated the British to win the American Revolution; George Washington was the first president of the United States; fifty states make up the United States of America. These are all facts. No
40 sensible person would disagree that each statement is true. Each claim can be verified through research and the study of documentary sources.

Opinions are beliefs people have
45 based on how they interpret certain facts. Opinions are open to argument and can be disputed: The American Revolution was the most important event in world history; George
50 Washington was the greatest president the United States has ever had; the United States was wrong to become involved in the Vietnam War. These statements are opinions. Some people
55 might agree with these statements—but agreeing with them doesn't make them facts.

When studying both primary and secondary sources, historians must
60 remember that people view history differently depending on their historical points of view. A person's gender, race, or economic or social standing often determines how he or she interprets
65 history. When studying documentary

sources, it is important that a historian knows something about the person or people responsible for the source. The point of view of this person could have
70 affected his or her reporting or interpretation of the event that was documented. If a historian relies on a primary or secondary source without taking into account that source's point
75 of view, he or she might come to an incomplete or inaccurate understanding of history.

Good historians understand that several things can affect a person's point
80 of view. One is nationalism. Nationalism is pride in your country. Being proud of your country can be a good thing. However, nationalism can also influence the way in which people
85 view history. A person who is a strong nationalist will record the actions of his or her country as being positive acts, whereas someone more objective might document the same event or period in a
90 negative light. For example, Frederick Jackson Turner was a white historian and a strong US nationalist. He viewed western settlement during the 1800s as a glorious period in US history. He taught
95 that the United States was a strong nation because of its efforts to conquer western territories all the way to the Pacific Ocean. Many Native Americans, however, view the
100 westward expansion of the United States as a tragic time. Native Americans suffered during this period when white settlers took their tribal lands and destroyed many Native
105 Americans' way of life. Native Americans view the same historical period differently than white nationalists like Frederick Jackson Turner.

110 Through their study of the past, historians discover and ultimately teach valuable lessons. By understanding the causes of past events, they make it possible for people to learn from earlier
115 people's mistakes, equipping today's generation to approach the future wiser and better prepared to make the world a better place.

9. The passage suggests that the author wants readers to:

   A. understand why history is important to them.

   B. know how good historians study history.

   C. learn to form their own historical opinions.

   D. be suspicious of most historical research.

10. Based on the passage, why most likely would African Americans and European Americans have different understandings of the history of the 1960s civil rights movement?

   F. Different groups cannot be affected by the same historical period.

   G. One group would likely focus on facts, while the other would focus on opinions.

   H. There would not be enough documentary sources for both groups to study.

   J. The two groups regard the same period from two different points of view.

6

11. According to the passage, a good historian does which of the following?

   A. Distinguishes between fact and opinion
   B. Ignores the influences of historical point of view
   C. Resists forming opinions about historical data
   D. Relies on primary rather than secondary sources

12. Which of the following does the passage suggest might create a misunderstanding of the reasons for a historical event?

   F. Studying facts about the event
   G. Forgetting to consider nationalism
   H. Relying purely on secondary sources
   J. Failing to dismiss certain points of view

13. According to the passage, the work of historians leads to:

   A. valuable lessons regarding the future.
   B. inaccurate information that hurts society.
   C. more opinions than facts.
   D. distorted ideas about nationalism.

14. Based on the passage, a journal dating back to the Colonial Period definitely would serve:

   F. as a source of many important facts.
   G. to provide mostly opinions.
   H. as a primary source for study.
   J. to correct a historical point of view.

15. In the passage, Frederick Jackson Turner serves as an example of someone who:

   A. held a certain historical point of view.
   B. favored facts more than opinions.
   C. provided historians with primary sources.
   D. did not consider facts when studying history.

16. According to the passage, which of the following items would serve as an example of a secondary source?

   F. An interview with someone who took part in a historical event
   G. A painting created during a certain historical period
   H. A love letter written by a historical figure
   J. A book written by a professor about a historical figure

Diagnostic Test

Passage III

Directions: Read the passage below. Then answer the questions that follow it. Choose the best answer to each question based on your reading of the passage. You may refer to the passage as often as needed.

HUMANITIES: This passage is an excerpt from "A South African Storm," a personal memoir by Peace Corps volunteer Allison Howard (*Crossing Cultures with the Peace Corps*, www.peacecorps.gov).

It's a Saturday afternoon in January in South Africa. When I begin the 45-minute walk to the shops for groceries, I can hear thunder cracking in the
5 distance up the mountain in Mageobaskloof. But at 4 p.m. the sky is still light and bright and I am sure—famous last words—I will be fine without an umbrella.

10 Just the basics: eggs, bread, Diet Coke in a bag slung into the crook of my elbow. Halfway from town, two black South African women—domestic workers in the homes of white Afrikaner
15 families—stop me with wide smiles. They know me; I'm the only white person in town who walks everywhere, as they do. They chatter quickly in northern Sotho: "Missus, you must go
20 fast. *Pula e tla na!* The rain, it comes!" They like me, and it feels very important to me that they do. *"Yebo, yebo, mma,"* I say—Yes, it's true—and I hurry along in flip-flops, quickening my pace,
25 feeling good about our brief but neighborly conversation. These are Venda women.

My black South African friends tell me it's easy to tell a Venda from a
30 Shangaan from a Xhosa from a Pedi. "These ones from Venda, they have wide across the nose and high in the cheekbones," they say. But I don't see it; I'm years away from being able to
35 distinguish the nuances of ethnicity. Today, I know these women are Vendas simply because of their clothing: bright stripes of green and yellow and black fabric tied at one shoulder and hanging
40 quite like a sack around their bodies. They've already extended a kindness to me by speaking in northern Sotho. It's not their language but they know I don't speak a word of Afrikaans (though they
45 don't understand why; Afrikaans is the language of white people). They know I struggle with Sotho and they're trying to help me learn. So they speak Sotho to me and they're delighted and amused by
50 my fumbling responses. And I am, quite simply, delighted by their delight.

The Venda ladies are right: the rain, it comes. Lightly at first, and by habit I begin trotting to hurry my way home.
55 Just a little rain at first and there are plenty of us out in it. I can see others up ahead on the street and others still just leaving the shops to get back before the real rain begins.

60 The people who are walking along this swath of tar road are black. Black people don't live in this neighborhood—or in my town at all, for the most part. They work and board here
65 as domestic workers, nannies, gardeners. Their families live in black

8

townships and rural villages—some just outside of my town; others far away, in places like Venda.

[70] Today, we're walking together in the rain, and I'm quickening my pace because—after all, *it's raining*. That's what you do in the rain. And even though it's coming down noticeably [75] harder, it's 80 degrees and I'm not cold, I'm just wet. My hair is stuck to my forehead and my T-shirt is soaked ... and I'm the only one running for cover. And I think: So what? It's just water and in [80] the middle of the January summer, it's warm, refreshing water. Why run? Why do we run from the rain?

In my life back in the United States, I might run because I was carrying a [85] leather handbag, or because I wore an outfit that shouldn't get wet. I would run because rain dishevels and messes things up. Mostly though, we run because we just do; it's a habit. I've [90] done it a hundred times: running to my car or the subway station with a newspaper sheltering my head. I have never *not* quickened my pace in the rain until today.

[95] It took all of my 27 years and a move to Africa, where I don't have a leather handbag to shelter or a pretty outfit to protect. I'm wearing an old cotton skirt and a T-shirt, and I'm [100] drenched, and I love it. I learn things here in the most ordinary circumstances. And I feel like a smarter, better woman today because I got groceries in the rain.

17. In the passage, the phrase "famous last words" (line 8) is used to communicate that:

   A. these are the last words the narrator speaks before dying.

   B. these are the final words the narrator shares before shopping.

   C. the narrator has assumed something due to a misjudgment.

   D. the narrator has quoted someone who is very well known.

18. According to the passage, Venda, Shangaan, and Xhosa are different:

   F. languages.

   G. ethnic groups.

   H. regions of South Africa.

   J. geographic features.

19. The fact that the narrator is the "only white person in town who walks everywhere, as they do" (lines 16–18) suggests that:

   A. white South Africans tend to have more resources than black South Africans.

   B. black South Africans prefer walking to driving everywhere in their cars.

   C. the narrator resents the fact that she has to walk, unlike other white people.

   D. most white South Africans are not comfortable walking all over town.

Diagnostic Test

20. Which of the following generalizations can the reader draw from the passage?

    F. Poor black South Africans often work for white South Africans.

    G. South Africans are more used to the rain than North Americans are.

    H. South Africans tend to work in the neighborhoods in which they live.

    J. People who walk in the rain instead of running tend to be smarter.

21. This passage recounting the author's time in South Africa:

    A. exposes racial injustices in South Africa.

    B. is told from a first-person point of view.

    C. makes a social statement about the need to help blacks in South Africa.

    D. implies that North American culture is superior to South African culture.

22. Based on the passage, how do the black South Africans who know the narrator feel about her?

    F. They resent her because she is white.

    G. They look to her to teach them things.

    H. They are cautious and suspicious of her.

    J. They accept and are friendly toward her.

23. According to the passage, why does the narrator still run when she is caught in the rain?

    A. She is trying to protect her handbag.

    B. She is trying to protect her groceries.

    C. She is running out of habit.

    D. She is running because she's cold.

24. When the author writes "I feel like a smarter, better woman today because I got groceries in the rain" (lines 102–104) she is referring to the fact that she:

    F. has overcome obstacles to go to the store and back in the rain.

    G. has changed her old behaviors by understanding a new culture.

    H. now knows how to recognize the signs that the rains will come.

    J. is able to improve her conversational skills in speaking Sotho.

25. Based on the passage, the preoccupation with material possessions often leads Americans to:

    A. rush about when they should enjoy the moment.

    B. drive cars when they could just as easily walk.

    C. avoid visiting places with different cultures.

    D. forget to extend kindness to others.

10

DIAGNOSTIC TEST EVALUATION CHART

Directions: On the following chart, circle the question numbers that you answered incorrectly, and evaluate the results. Then turn to the appropriate topics (organized by chapters), read the explanations, and complete the exercises to sharpen your skills in these areas. Review other chapters as necessary. Finally, complete the two Practice Tests at the end of the book to further prepare yourself for the PLAN Reading Test.

****Note that some questions appear in more than one chapter, indicating an overlap in skills needed to answer the question.

Chapter	Questions
Chapter 2: Main Idea, Supporting Details, and Author's Approach	1, 3, 7, 8, 9, 11, 16, 18, 19, 21, 25
Chapter 3: Reading for Relationships	2, 10, 12, 13, 15, 20
Chapter 4: Interpreting Words and Phrases	4, 6, 17, 24
Chapter 5: Generalizations and Conclusions	5, 10, 14, 22, 23, 25

Diagnostic Test

Chapter 1
What to Expect and How to Prepare

WHAT TO EXPECT ON THE PLAN READING TEST

This book focuses on the **Reading Test** portion of PLAN, the test which many US students take to help prepare them to take the ACT. The ACT is one of two major college assessment exams (the other being the SAT).

TEST CONTENT

Students will have **20 minutes to complete the reading portion of the test**. The test consists of **25 questions** designed to measure your skills in reading comprehension. The exam tests your reading skills by requiring you to read and process materials from various subject areas and then answer corresponding questions. The exam *does not* test knowledge outside of the written passages, vocabulary taken out of context, or rules of formal logic.

The PLAN Reading Test consists of **three passages** similar to what you would encounter in your high school curriculum. The test passages include one prose fiction passage, one passage dealing with the humanities, and one passage dealing with the social sciences.

Prose Fiction	The prose fiction passage will be an intact short story or excerpt from a short story or novel.
Humanities	The humanities passage will consists of material such as portions of memoirs or personal essays and content dealing with art, architecture, film, philosophy, language, music, literary criticism, radio, television, drama, dance, and ethics.
Social Sciences	The social sciences passage will consist of material addressing subject matter such as anthropology, archaeology, a biography, business, economics, education, geography, history, political science, psychology, and sociology.

You do not need to be knowledgeable about the subject matter of a passage beyond what is written in the passage. However, you do need to read each passage carefully. Remember, the purpose of the PLAN Reading Test is to measure your reading comprehension. Test questions are designed to determine if you understand what you have read.

What to Expect and How to Prepare

TYPES OF QUESTIONS

The passages included on the PLAN Reading Test vary in their levels of difficulty. Some passages are *Uncomplicated*, requiring very basic skills to understand and effectively answer the corresponding questions. Other passages are *More Challenging* and require greater ability to recognize and understand figurative language, intricate structure, complex interactions, more extensive data, and/or some difficult context-dependent words. Finally, some passages are *Complex* and require understanding ambiguous language and literary devices, complex and subtle interactions between characters, more challenging context-specific vocabulary, messages and/or meanings that are embedded rather than explicit, sizable amounts of data, demanding words and phrases, and/or intricate explanations of processes or events.

Skills assessed by the test include the following:

- Referring to details within the passage
- Drawing conclusions based on available information
- Making comparisons and generalizations

You may be asked to do the following:

- Identify the main idea and/or supporting details.
- Understand the correct sequence of events.
- Identify the author's main purpose.
- Understand and recognize cause-effect relationships.
- Understand the implication of a certain word or phrase.
- Understand figurative language.
- Use context to understand the figurative or nonfigurative meaning of a word.
- Compare characters, circumstances, scenarios, or facts.
- Draw simple generalizations and conclusions about characters, people, ideas, and so on.
- Draw subtle generalizations and conclusions about characters, people, ideas, and so on.
- Use information from a section of a passage to draw generalizations and conclusions about people, ideas, and so on.

DIAGNOSTIC AND PRACTICE TESTS

The Diagnostic Test at the beginning and Practice Tests 1 and 2 at the end of this book are simulated PLAN Reading Tests. They are the same length and contain passages and questions comparable to those you will see on the reading portion of the actual PLAN assessment. Review your scores on these tests with your teacher or tutor to determine if there are any skill areas you need to hone before taking the PLAN.

Chapter 1

For practice with other sections of the PLAN, refer to these titles from American Book Company:

PLAN English Test Preparation Guide

PLAN Mathematics Test Preparation Guide

PLAN Science Test Preparation Guide

FREQUENTLY ASKED QUESTIONS

What is the PLAN?

The PLAN is a national test taken by many high school students in tenth grade to help prepare them to take the ACT. The ACT is a college admission examination which is accepted by most US colleges and universities. The exam measures the knowledge, understanding, and skills that you have gained throughout your education.

Note: It is always a good idea to do your homework ahead of time to know which of the two major college assessments—ACT or SAT—the schools you are most interested in prefer. Many prefer one or the other; some may require both.

How long is the exam?

The full PLAN assessment includes 145 multiple-choice questions. It covers four subjects: English, Mathematics, Reading, and Science. The total testing time for all four portions is 115 minutes (30 minutes for English, 40 minutes for Mathematics, 20 minutes for Reading, and 25 minutes for Science).

When do I take the PLAN, and is there a fee?

As mentioned earlier, PLAN is a test intended to prepare tenth graders to eventually take the ACT during their eleventh and/or twelfth grade year. Any students interested in taking the PLAN should check with their teacher and/or guidance counselor *prior to or at the start of their tenth-grade year* to learn the dates that the exam will be administered, how to properly register, and what fees may apply.

For more details about PLAN testing, you can visit the assessment website at www.actstudent.org/plan.

TIPS FOR PLAN PREPARATION AND TESTING

The PLAN measures your overall learning, so if you have paid attention in school, you should do well! It would be difficult (if not impossible!) to "cram" for an exam as comprehensive as the PLAN test. However, you can study wisely by using a PLAN-specific guide (like this book) and practice answering questions of the type that will be asked on the PLAN (included in this book). Additional practice tests are available online from ACT, Inc., at www.actstudent.org/plan/pdf/sample.pdf.

What to Expect and How to Prepare

PREPARING FOR THE PLAN

- **Believe in yourself!** Attitude plays a big part in how well you do in anything. Keep your thoughts positive. Tell yourself you will do well on the exam.

- **Be prepared**. Get a good night's sleep the day before your exam. Eat a well-balanced meal, one that contains plenty of proteins and carbohydrates, prior to your exam. Obviously, keep in mind any physical traits, food allergies, and so on that may be specific to your situation. Stick to any special dietary plan you follow. The bottom line is, make sure you have the rest and nourishment you need so that you can feel good and remain confident and focused.

- **Arrive early**. Allow yourself at least fifteen to twenty minutes to find your room and get settled. Then you can relax before the exam, so you won't feel rushed.

- **Relax!** Some students become overly worried about exams. Some even suffer from what is commonly known as *test anxiety*. Students who have test anxiety sometimes perspire heavily, experience an upset stomach, or have shortness of breath before and/or while taking the test. If you feel any of these symptoms before the test, talk to a close friend or see a counselor for ways to deal with test anxiety. Here are some quick ways to relieve test anxiety:

    - Imagine yourself in your favorite place. Let yourself sit and relax.

    - Do a body scan. Tense and relax each part of your body starting with your toes and ending with your forehead.

    - Use the 3-12-6 method of relaxation when you feel stress. Inhale slowly for three seconds. Hold your breath for twelve seconds, and then exhale slowly for six seconds.

TAKING THE PLAN

- Carefully **read the instructions** in the PLAN test booklet. You can read these instructions ahead of time at www.actstudent.org/plan to make sure that you understand them. You also will find version of these instructions at the beginning of each practice passage in this book.

- Once the test administrator tells you that you may open your test booklet, thoroughly **read the directions for a test section** before reading its corresponding passage or answering its questions.

- **Read each question carefully**, and use your best approach for answering the questions. Some test-takers like to skim the questions and answers before reading the passage. Others prefer to read the passage before looking at the answers. Use whichever approach works best for you.

- **Answer each question** on the exam. Your score is based on the number of questions answered correctly. There is no penalty for guessing, but every spot left blank is automatically a zero. So take a chance on an answer, even if you are not sure. It might help, and it can't hurt.

    - If you are uncertain about an answer, **take an educated guess**. Eliminate choices that are definitely wrong, and then choose from the remaining answers.

Chapter 1

- **Use your answer sheet correctly.** Make sure the number on your question matches the number on your answer sheet. If you need to change your answer, erase it completely. Use a no. 2 pencil, and make sure the answers are dark. The computerized scanner may skip over answers that are too light.

- **Check your answers.** If you finish a test before time is called, review your exam to make sure you have chosen the best responses. Change answers only if you are sure they are wrong.

- Be sure to **pace yourself**. Since you will have a limited amount of time, be careful not to spend too much time on one passage, leaving no time to complete the rest of the test. Listen for the announcement of five minutes remaining on each test.

- When time is called for each test, **put your pencil down**. If you continue to write or erase after time has been called, you run the risk of being dismissed and your test being disqualified from scoring.

What to Look for When You Take the PLAN Reading Test

The PLAN Reading Test has **three passages**: one focuses on prose fiction, one on the humanities, and one on an area of the social sciences.

- **Read each whole passage** quickly but carefully. Questions may ask you about parts of the passage and may refer to particular paragraphs. Ultimately, the questions all rely on your understanding of the passage as a whole.

- Pay attention to the "**advance organizers**," the title and brief explanation at the beginning of each passage. These brief introductions tell the reader which area the passage is covering (prose fiction, humanities, social science), what the passage is about, and where it comes from. It also may provide some additional information that will be helpful in understanding the passage.

- Don't get tripped up by your existing knowledge about the topic of a passage. Remember that the Reading Test does not measure your subject-matter knowledge—it **assesses how well you** *read*. This is why many questions begin, "According to the passage…" or with some similar phrase. Say, for example, you have an interest in architecture and see a humanities passage addressing that topic. Don't jump to conclusions based on the knowledge you already have! Be sure to *read what the passage says* rather than relying on what you already know. The author's conclusions may not coincide with what you have learned in the past. Answer the questions according to the content of the passage, not your own expertise.

- **Read the answer choices carefully.** Although there are no "trick questions" on the PLAN Reading Test, there may be subtle differences in answers. If two answers seem to make sense to you, read them again, determine how they differ, and decide which one *best* answers the question. There is **always only one correct answer** to each test question.

What to Expect and How to Prepare

HOW THE PLAN READING TEST WILL LOOK

The PLAN Reading Test will measure your reading comprehension by requiring you to derive meaning from several written passages based on what you have read. You must be able to derive the passages' meaning (1) by referring to what is explicitly stated in the written content and (2) by using reasoning to draw conclusions, comparisons, and generalizations and determine implied meanings.

The test will include three passages. Each passage will fall under one of three umbrella subject areas: **prose fiction**, **humanities**, and **social sciences**. The passages in this book cannot represent every type of passage you could possibly see, but they will provide practice for reading and for answering the types of questions that will be on the test.

No matter what the subject of the passage, you are likely to find the following types of corresponding questions:

Main Ideas: Main idea questions will test your ability to grasp the main idea of what you've read. In other words, you are asked to recognize the author's intent in writing the passage. What is the author's purpose? What is he or she trying to say? Is the author trying to prove a point or simply trying to share information? Is the author setting a scene or telling a story? Some questions might ask you to identify the main idea of the whole passage. Others might ask you to focus on a portion of the passage. Here are a couple of tips for main idea questions.

1. Ask yourself, "What is the author saying? What does he or she want me to know and walk away with when I've read this passage?"

2. It is important to remember that *the main idea might or might not be explicitly stated*. Some main ideas are implied.

3. Some questions might ask about "one of the main ideas" of a paragraph or passage.

4. Try to rule out choices that are either supporting ideas or misstatements of what the passage says.

Supporting Details: Supporting details can be facts, references, descriptions, and so on in the passage which help the author make his or her overall argument, illustrate a point, set a scene, draw some conclusion, or imply what the author wants the reader to infer from the passage or a portion of the passage. Questions that ask you to recognize supporting details may point out a fact, conclusion, or inference in or from some portion of the passage and require you to identify a supporting detail in the passage that supports or makes the fact, conclusion, or inference evident.

Author's Approach: Some questions will require you to analyze and recognize the author's approach. What point of view did the writer use (first, second, third)? Did the author write an argumentative piece, informative piece, or literary piece? Does the author rely on symbolism, personification, dialogue, and so forth? Does the writer use descriptive or figurative language? These types of questions ask you to recognize the author's method of writing.

Chapter 1

Sequential Questions: These types of questions ask you to identify the sequence of events in a passage. The question might deal with the chronological sequence (what event occurred first, last, and so on chronologically), or it may simply ask you to identify the sequence of events or details in the passage itself (what event or detail is mentioned first, last, or so on in the passage regardless of where it fell chronologically).

Comparative Relationships: Questions dealing with comparative relationships ask you to identify or interpret similarities or differences between ideas, events, characters, and so on. Some are straightforward questions about comparisons and contrasts presented in a passage, while others require you to perceive subtle similarities and differences.

Cause-Effect Relationships: These types of questions may ask about the causes of an event or about the effects of something happening. For prose fiction, this can relate to how characters behave or are affected by an event or certain circumstances. In nonfiction passages, it may refer to processes or the impact of historical events or trends.

Interpreting Words and Phrases: Some questions will require you to determine the meaning of words or phrases in context. In other words, you will need to decipher their meaning based on the way they are used in the passage.

Generalizations and Conclusions: These questions ask you to look concisely at what you just read and make a general observation. Questions may ask you to conclude something or to make an inference about an event, idea, or character.

Read the following excerpt from a passage, try answering the questions that follow on your own, and then study the explanations about which answer is the correct one and why.

SAMPLE PASSAGE WITH EXPLANATIONS

(Notice that the passage begins with an "advanced organizer," letting you know that the passage is a Social Science passage.)

SOCIAL SCIENCES: This passage is an essay entitled "Why Is There So Much Fighting in Northern Ireland?"

Conflict has been a way of life for centuries in Ireland, the island off the western shore of England. The Anglo-Normans first invaded the island in 1167, and there has been unrest ever since. To understand this or any ongoing conflict, it is important to learn about its history.

Ireland has tried to free itself of British rule for many years. There were many uprisings, especially in the eighteenth and nineteenth centuries. All this time, the Irish people fought a common enemy: the British invaders. But by the end of the nineteenth century, the Irish began fighting among themselves. They started to disagree about having home rule (become an independent nation). In the North (which was now industrialized, and where many Protestants lived), the "Unionists" wanted to be united with Britain. After all, it was good for business. They were also afraid that independence would bring influence from Rome, the seat of Catholicism, because Ireland's capital was Dublin (in the South, mainly a farming area where many Catholics lived).

In 1912, Ireland finally became independent on paper. However, the First World War put everything on hold. By the end of the war, no real steps had been taken. So the Irish Republican Army (IRA) was formed and started to attack the occupying British. In 1920, Britain set up a parliament in Ireland. They thought this would make it seem as though Ireland had its own government. Meanwhile it would help the British control Ireland. The Unionists accepted this. But the Nationalists were determined to gain real independence.

Finally, an Irish Free State was established in 1921. This step officially divided Ireland's thirty-two counties. The twenty-six counties in the South became the Republic of Ireland. The remaining six counties in the North were now called Northern Ireland. Of course, this did not mean everyone was happy or that all Irish citizens lived where their views were accepted.

There was much discrimination against Catholics in Northern Ireland. As a result, civil rights protests began in the 1960s. People there were inspired by the civil rights movement in the United States. But in Northern Ireland, the movement became ever more violent. A crucial moment came during the infamous Battle of the Bogside (a Catholic section of Londonderry) in 1969. To stop this two-day riot, the Irish Prime Minister asked for military help from Britain. British force was again brought in, and British troops remain in Northern Ireland to this day.

Over the years, many more horrible clashes have happened. An example is Bloody Sunday in 1972, when British troops, claiming they were fired on
75 first, killed more than a dozen protesters. Many solutions also have been tried. One example is the Belfast Agreement of 1999 that tried to transition troops out of Northern
80 Ireland, but unsuccessfully. There always seems to be some part of the treaties that favors one side or the other. Still, everyone continues trying to find a way to stop the fighting.

85 The BBC–Northern Ireland reported at the end of 2004 that most citizens just want to get on with their lives. People were asked how they feel about the Protestant–Catholic problem.
90 Responses showed that most people do not see the other side as the enemy. For example, nine out of ten people do not care whether their doctor is Protestant or Catholic. Over 90 percent would
95 consider selling their home to someone from the other tradition. Many peace projects have started, and the governments continue to negotiate. Everyone hopes that one day both sides
100 will find the perfect balance to put an end to the fighting in Northern Ireland.

1. According to the passage, which of the following occurred first?

   A. The formation of the Irish Republican Army
   B. Disagreements among the Irish about independence
   C. The Battle of the Bogside
   D. Bloody Sunday

Answer B is correct. This question is asking you to identify which of the listed events occurred first. If you read the passage closely, you note that disagreements among the Irish about independence arose before the formation of the IRA. (Answer A is eliminated.) They also arose before the Battle of the Bogside. (Answer C is eliminated.) And they arose before the occurrence of Bloody Sunday. (Answer D is eliminated.) Therefore, disagreements among the Irish about independence arose first.

2. Based on the passage, we can infer that:

   F. ordinary citizens can get along for the most part.
   G. there are fewer Catholics than Protestants in Ireland.
   H. the 1969 arrival of British troops helped end conflict.
   J. the IRA is determined to keep the peace in Ireland.

Answer F is correct. This question is asking you to comprehend explicitly stated information in the passage to draw a conclusion that will enable you to infer something that is not explicitly stated. You know from the passage that Southern Ireland is mostly Catholic and that there are many Catholics in Northern Ireland as well. Therefore, you cannot correctly infer that there are fewer Catholics in Ireland than Protestants. (Answer G is eliminated.) You also know from reading the passage that the arrival of British troops contributed to the ongoing conflict, rather than helping end it. (Answer H is eliminated.) The passage also makes it clear that the purpose of the IRA is to violently resist the British, not promote peace. (Answer J is eliminated.) However,

What to Expect and How to Prepare

the final paragraph states that most citizens just want to get on with their lives and aren't as concerned about differences dividing Catholics and Protestants. Therefore, we can infer that ordinary citizens can get along for the most part.

3. Which of the following resulted from the establishment of the Irish Free State?
   A. Anglo-Normans invaded the island.
   B. A lasting peace treaty finally was forged.
   C. The British set up a parliament in Ireland.
   D. Ireland was divided into two countries.

Answer D is correct. This question is asking you to identify what occurred as a result of the establishment of the Irish Free State. A close reading of the passage reveals that the Anglo-Normans invaded long before the Irish Free State was ever established. Therefore, this could not have been a result of the Irish Free State. (Answer A is eliminated.) You also learn from the passage that no lasting peace has been established in Ireland because the author states at the end of the passage that "one day" both sides will find a way to put an end to the fighting. (Answer B is eliminated.) You learn from reading the passage that Great Britain established a parliament in Ireland in 1920, before the Irish Free State was established in 1921. Since the parliament was established first, it could not have resulted from the Irish Free State. (Answer C is eliminated.) Finally, the passage clearly states that the establishment of the Irish Free State officially divided Ireland into the independent nations of Northern and Southern Ireland.

4. The passage suggests that:
   F. military force is needed greatly in Northern Ireland.
   G. the conflict is based largely on religious differences.
   H. dividing the country has helped decrease the fighting.
   J. the IRA has accomplished what it set out to do.

Answer G is correct. This question is asking you to infer something based on explicit information in the passage. The passage clearly states that there has been a military presence in Ireland for many years, yet the conflict does not end. This would suggest that military force is not the answer to ending the conflict. (Answer F is eliminated.) In 1921, the country was officially divided. However, this did not end the conflict. This would suggest that dividing the country failed to decrease the fighting. (Answer H is eliminated.) According to the passage, the IRA's purpose was to use force to drive the British from Ireland. However, the passage clearly states that "British troops remain in Northern Ireland to this day." This shows that the IRA has not yet accomplished its goal. (Answer J is eliminated.) The passage makes constant references to the conflicts between Protestants and Catholics. This suggests that the conflict is based largely on religious differences.

5. According to the passage, most members of the IRA probably tend to be:
   A. British.
   B. Protestants.
   C. Nationalists.
   D. Unionists.

Answer C is correct. This question is asking you to draw a conclusion based on information explicitly stated in the passage. The passage tells you that the IRA was established for the purpose of fighting against the British in Ireland. Therefore, you can conclude that most members of the IRA are not British. (Answer A is eliminated.) The passage also tells you that the areas of Ireland that have wanted to remain loyal to Britain are areas with high numbers of Protestants. Therefore, you can conclude that Protestants tend to be loyal to Britain. Therefore, you can conclude that most members of the IRA are not Protestant. (Answer B is eliminated.) The passage also says that the Unionists wanted to remain united with Britain. Since this goal is the exact opposite of the IRA's, you can conclude that most members of the IRA are not Unionists. (Answer D is eliminated.) However, the passage tells you that Nationalists were devoted to Ireland's "real independence." Since this goal goes hand-in-hand with the goal of the IRA, you can conclude that members of the IRA are Nationalists. (Answer C is correct.)

6. The author clearly believes that:
   F. it is important to understand the past if we hope to understand the present.
   G. Great Britain was wrong to establish its rule over Ireland.
   H. the IRA is justified in using violent resistance against the British.
   J. Ireland will one day be united and free.

Answer F is correct. This question is asking you to identify something the author believes based on what he or she has stated in the passage. Although you might draw a conclusion that it was wrong for Great Britain to establish its rule in Ireland, the author does not clearly state this nor does he or she make this argument. (Answer G is eliminated.) Although you might draw a conclusion that the IRA is justified in using violence to resist British rule, the author does not clearly state this nor does he or she make this argument. (Answer H is eliminated.) Although you might believe that Ireland will one day be united and free, the author does not state this nor does he or she make this argument. (Answer J is eliminated.) However, the author does state in the opening paragraph: "To understand this or any ongoing conflict, it is important to learn about history." Therefore, you can conclude that the author believes it is important to understand the past if we hope to understand the present.

7. The author's purpose is to:
   A. argue for the Irish people's right to self-rule.
   B. present evidence as to why some countries have violent conflicts.
   C. help readers understand the Irish–British conflict.
   D. recite the history of the Irish–British conflict.

Answer C is correct. While you might conclude that the Irish people have a right to self-rule, the author does not state this nor does he or she offer any argument trying to persuade readers that this is true. (Answer A is eliminated.) Although the author gives reasons for Ireland's conflict, he or she does not discuss other countries or suggest that the reasons for Ireland's conflict are consistent with conflicts in other countries. (Answer B is eliminated.) Although the author does recite portions of Ireland's history, he or she implies that the purpose of knowing the historical facts is to help readers understand the ongoing conflict, not simply to educate them regarding Irish history. (Answer D is eliminated.)

8. Which of the following sentences best describes the Catholic civil rights movement that arose in Northern Ireland?

    F. It closely resembled the civil rights movement that took place in the United States.

    G. It was inspired by the US civil rights movement but was not as peaceful.

    H. It lasted only a short while because its nonviolent protests were ineffective.

    J. It inspired the civil rights movement that later took place in the United States.

Answer G is correct. The author says that the Catholic civil rights movement was inspired by the US civil rights movement, "but" that it grew ever more violent. The fact that he or she uses the word *but* implies that the US civil rights movement was not as violent. Therefore, the Catholic civil rights movement did not resemble the US civil rights movement. (Answer F is eliminated.) The author does not state how long the civil rights movement lasted, but does imply that it was several years. Nor does he or she make any statement regarding its effectiveness. (Answer H is eliminated.) The passage clearly states that the Catholic civil rights movement was inspired by the civil rights movement in the United States, rather than vice versa. (Answer J is eliminated.) However, while the author does clearly state that the Irish–Catholic civil rights movement was inspired by the US civil rights movement, he or she also implies that it was more violent. It was not peaceful.

READING FORWARD

Now that you know some basic facts about the PLAN Reading Test and have an idea of what to expect, you are ready to read the rest of this book. Each chapter will address a specific aspect of comprehensive reading and will give you a chance to practice and hone these skills. So read on, and be confident—this book will help you review the skills you need to master every aspect of this test.

Chapter 2
Understanding the Main Idea, Supporting Details, and Author's Approach

Some questions on the PLAN Reading Test will require you to be able to identify and summarize **main ideas, basic events, and details** that are stated or implied in a passage. You will also need to identify the **author's purpose and approach**. You need to choose the answer that best identifies an idea (often the main idea), or the answer that best summarizes an event or detail mentioned or implied in the text. Main idea, supporting details, and author's approach questions on the PLAN Reading Test earn points based on the following point ranges. These begin with fundamental skills in identifying these elements and progress to inference skills in more complex reading.

13–15	Recognize a clear intent of an author or narrator in uncomplicated literary narratives
	Locate basic facts (e.g., names, dates, events) clearly stated in a passage
16–19	Identify a clear main idea or purpose of straightforward paragraphs in uncomplicated literary narratives
	Locate simple details at the sentence and paragraph level in uncomplicated passages
	Recognize a clear function of a part of an uncomplicated passage
20–23	Infer the main idea or purpose of straightforward paragraphs in uncomplicated literary narratives
	Understand the overall approach taken by an author or narrator (e.g., point of view, kinds of evidence used) in uncomplicated passages
	Locate important details in uncomplicated passages
	Make simple inferences about how details are used in passages
24–27	Identify a clear main idea or purpose of any paragraph or paragraphs in uncomplicated passages
	Infer the main idea or purpose of straightforward paragraphs in more challenging passages
	Summarize basic events and ideas in more challenging passages
	Understand the overall approach taken by an author or narrator (e.g., point of view, kinds of evidence used) in more challenging passages
	Locate important details in more challenging passages
	Locate and interpret minor or subtly stated details in uncomplicated passages
	Discern which details, though they may appear in different sections throughout a passage, support important points in more challenging passages
28–32	Infer the main idea or purpose of more challenging passages or their paragraphs
	Summarize events and ideas in virtually any passage
	Understand the overall approach taken by an author or narrator (e.g., point of view, kinds of evidence used) in virtually any passage
	Locate and interpret minor or subtly stated details in more challenging passages
	Use details from different sections of some complex informational passages to support a specific point or argument

Understanding the Main Idea, Supporting Details, and Author's Approach

In this chapter, you will review how to recognize directly stated and implied main ideas and supporting details. You will also review how to identify an author's approach based on the information available in a passage.

MAIN IDEA

The **main idea** of a passage is the central point or controlling idea. In other words, what does the author of the passage want readers to understand after reading? Some questions also will refer to the **purpose** of a passage. This is related, referring to the reason the author wrote it. In this case, think back to the purposes for writing: to inform, to persuade, to entertain, and so on. You will read more about the author's intent (purpose) under the "Author's Approach" section later in this chapter.

DIRECTLY STATED MAIN IDEA

Sometimes, **a main idea is directly stated** in a passage. It might be stated in the title of the passage or near the beginning or the end of the passage. Keep in mind that passages included on the PLAN Reading Test will not always give you the title of a passage.

Below is a passage in which the main idea is directly stated.

The Comeback of Rabies

Rabies, a deadly disease to both animals and humans, is on the increase in many areas of Florida. In fact, the number of reported human exposures to rabies has not been as high since the 1940s. This particular strain of
5   rabies was brought to Florida by Texas coyotes. Truckloads of these coyotes are imported into the state by hunting clubs and are used in fox hunts. The disease has always been found among wild animals, but the real problem is that fewer than half of all dogs, cats, and farm
10   animals have been vaccinated against it. In 2007, twenty cats, ten dogs, and three horses contracted rabies—an increase of 500 percent in the last five years. Domestic animals must be vaccinated, for they are the ones most likely to have contact with humans.

In the passage above, the main idea is directly stated. The main idea is that cases of rabies are spreading quickly in Florida. The title suggests the main idea of the passage. In addition, the author begins the passage by stating that rabies is on the increase in many areas of Florida. The author then uses the remainder of the passage to offer evidence to support this point.

Chapter 2

Practice 1: Directly Stated Main Idea

Below is a passage in which the main idea is directly stated. Read the passage, and see if you can determine the main idea.

East Meets West

It is amazing how the Japanese have retained their cultural heritage while simultaneously integrating many parts of Western culture. One of the most popular adaptations is the style of dress. Most Japanese today wear Western-style clothing, such as
5 business suits, activewear, jeans, and T-shirts. Traditional clothing is often reserved for special occasions. Many Japanese also have adopted Western furnishings into their homes. It is not unusual to have a completely westernized home with only one traditional Japanese room. Western influences can be seen
10 throughout Japanese popular culture, such as fast-food restaurants, music, and movies.

The Japanese have also gained more time to devote to leisure. Surveys show that spending time with family, friends, home improvement, shopping, and gardening form the mainstream of leisure, together with
15 sports and travel. The number of Japanese making overseas trips has increased notably in recent years. Domestic travel, picnics, hiking, and cultural events rank high among favorite activities.

Japan is a land with a vibrant and fascinating history, varied culture, traditions, and customs that are hundreds of years old, yet segments of its society and economy are as new
20 as the hottest mp3s.

1. Which statement best describes the main idea of the passage?

   A. Gardening, sports, and travel are popular leisure activities in Japan.

   B. Japanese people are very fond of Westerners and welcome them to their country.

   C. American culture now dominates the Japanese way of life.

   D. Modern Japanese culture is a mix of traditions and Western trends.

Understanding the Main Idea, Supporting Details, and Author's Approach

Tips for Finding a Stated Main Idea
1. **Read the title.** The main topic for the paragraph or passage is often mentioned in the title. (Keep in mind that not all passages on the PLAN Reading Test will include a title.
2. **Read the entire paragraph or passage.** You'll get an overview of who or what the selection is all about.
3. **Read the first and last sentence of each paragraph.** Most of the key words and ideas will be stated in these places.
4. **Choose the answer that is the best statement or restatement of the paragraph or passage.** Your choice might contain the key words and/or concepts mentioned or contained in the title, the first sentences, or the last sentences of each paragraph or passage.

IMPLIED MAIN IDEA

Sometimes an author will not directly state the main idea of a passage in the title or the text. Instead, the **author implies the main idea** through what is in the text, expecting the reader to infer the passage's overall message.

An **implication** is a suggestion an author makes to communicate an indirect message or idea.

An **inference** is an educated guess a reader makes in order to understand an author's implied message or idea.

To help you understand the concept of an implied idea or message, let's consider the following sentence.

Outside, the wind blew bitterly cold, swirling the hard-falling snow.

In what season of the year does the scene described in the sentence above occur? It is winter, correct? How do you know? Nowhere does the author say it is winter. But the facts revealed in the sentence (the bitter cold, the hard-falling snow) *imply* that it is a winter scene. In the same way, an author can imply a main idea. You must consider the revealed facts and details of the passage to determine the overall implied main idea.

Keep in mind that you will often encounter only a portion of a passage on the PLAN. The main idea contained in the overall text of a book might have very little to do with the directly stated or implied main idea of the selected portion that you are reading and analyzing.

Chapter 2

Below is an example of a paragraph with an implied main idea.

Putting Energy Back into Your Life

Are you getting enough water? Think of your houseplants. When they are short on water, they droop. The same thing happens to you! Our bodies are made up of millions of cells; the principal part of these cells is
5   water. If the cells are low on water, you will function at less than full efficiency. Strive for drinking six to eight glasses of water each day.

What is the main idea of this paragraph?

A. Houseplants need water to live.

B. The body's cells are composed of a high percentage of water.

C. Our bodies are made up of millions of cells.

D. Drink water, because your body needs it to be efficient.

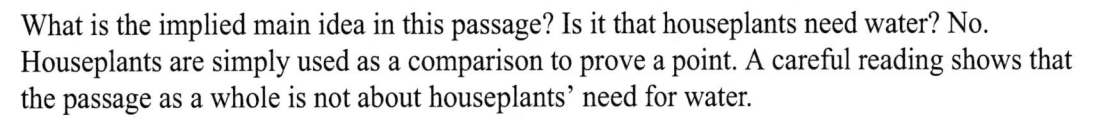

What is the implied main idea in this passage? Is it that houseplants need water? No. Houseplants are simply used as a comparison to prove a point. A careful reading shows that the passage as a whole is not about houseplants' need for water.

Is it about our bodies' cells being made up largely of water? No. While the author points out this fact, he or she merely does so to help support a larger point. The whole passage does not center on the role water plays in comprising human cells.

Look at the author's most important points to find the implied main idea. The author asks readers if they are getting enough water and points out the need for water (even houseplants droop without it; human cells that make up our bodies are comprised mostly of water). He or she concludes with the admonishment to drink six to eight glasses a day. You can conclude that the implied main idea is human beings should drink plenty of water.

Understanding the Main Idea, Supporting Details, and Author's Approach

Practice 2: Implied Main Idea

Below is a passage in which the main idea is implied rather than directly stated. Read the passage, and see if you can determine the main idea.

The Little Girl Who Could

Little Zack went outside and walked around the outdoor pool. There was something shiny in the bottom of the water, and when he looked closer, he fell into the pool. His sister, Penny, was making her little brother a peanut butter and jelly sandwich when she heard the splash. Seeing that her brother was nowhere in sight, Penny ran outside toward the pool.

5 When Penny arrived at the pool, she saw that her brother was motionless at the bottom of the pool. Quickly, Penny jumped in and brought Zack to the surface. Zack was not breathing and did not have a pulse. At nine years old, Penny had just taken a CPR course in her gym class at school. She immediately started doing what she had learned. She turned Zack's head upwards and began doing chest compressions and mouth-to-mouth
10 resuscitation. At this moment, Penny's mom came outside looking for her children. "Mom, call 911! Zack fell into the pool," Penny yelled. Penny's mom ran back inside and did what she was told. Penny's CPR had worked. Zack spit out the water quickly. Soon, Zack's pulse returned, and he was breathing on his own.

By the time the ambulance arrived, the color had returned to Zack's face, and he could
15 talk. The paramedics were amazed that this little girl had saved her brother's life. Instantly, Penny became a celebrity at school, and the school threw a party for her and the firemen who had taught her class CPR.

1. Which of the following statements best expresses the main idea of the passage?

   A. Zack should not have been walking so close to the pool.

   B. Everyone should learn CPR.

   C. Penny saved her brother's life.

   D. Penny's abilities as a strong swimmer saved Zack.

Chapter 2

SUPPORTING DETAILS

Some questions you encounter on the PLAN Reading Test will require you to recognize **simple details at the sentence and paragraph levels**. You should understand that **supporting details** are the facts, reasons, events, examples, and so on in a passage of text that support the passage's main idea. The supporting details make it possible for the reader to understand and/or accept the author's main idea.

Think of a table. The main idea is like the top of the table. The supporting details are like the legs. Just as the top of the table needs the legs to stand and be useful, so the main idea of a passage needs its supporting details to make sense or persuade the reader.

You will need to be able to **discern which details in a passage support important points**. Often, particularly in more-challenging passages, these details may be dispersed throughout the passage rather than being mentioned in succession or a clearly structured order.

BASIC FACTS

Basic facts are one form of supporting detail. Facts are pieces of information that can be proved; basic facts include names, dates, times, places, and so on. For example, if you are reading a passage on the Civil War, the questions you may have pertaining to basic facts might include the following:

When did the Civil War officially begin?

Where was the first battle fought?

What states comprised the Confederacy when the war began?

Who was president of the United States during the Civil War?

Many passages are organized around details and facts. The details are based on the *Five Ws and one H* (who, what, when, where, why, and how). When you are asked to find a detail or fact, you should scan or look for a specific piece of information by reading the passage again. For example, if you were given a passage on armadillos, you may be asked: What is an armadillo? Where do armadillos live? How big are armadillos? Why are armadillos a nuisance? When you read a question containing a *W* or *H* word, you will be looking for an answer with a fact or detail.

Tips for Locating Supporting Details
1. **Read the passage** carefully.
2. **Scan the passage** to answer *W* and *H* questions.
3. **Match key words** in your choice of answers with those in the passage.
4. **Always confirm your answer** by going back to the passage.

31

Understanding the Main Idea, Supporting Details, and Author's Approach

EVENTS AND EXAMPLES

Supporting information also appears in a passage in the form of **events or examples**. For instance, if an author's main idea is that chemical pollutants are responsible for higher rates of human illness, then he or she might use data showing that people exposed to pollutants get sick more often than those who are not exposed. The author might also refer to specific historical examples of people living in highly polluted areas who have shown signs of poor health. In this regard, if an author's main idea is that Martin Luther King Jr. is the most influential US citizen of the twentieth century, then he or she might recount historical examples of how African Americans were treated in the United States prior to the civil rights movement led by Dr. King.

Martin Luther King Jr.

Sometimes you might be asked to choose the best **summary of basic events and ideas**. Keep in mind that a summary is different from the main idea; in a summary, you give a brief synopsis of the events that propel the story, focusing on the most important ideas while leaving out minor details.

SUPPORTING DETAILS AND IMPLIED MAIN IDEAS

Supporting details help a reader properly infer an author's implied main idea. Think about the literary passage you read earlier, in which Penny saves her brother Zack. The main idea of the passage—Penny saves her brother's life—was not directly stated. However, you were able to infer that Penny had saved Zack's life because of the supporting details.

Penny sees that her brother is motionless at the bottom of the pool. (supporting detail)

Penny jumps in and brings Zack to the surface. (supporting detail)

Penny performs CPR. (supporting detail)

Zack's pulse returns, and he begins breathing on his own. (supporting detail)

Penny has saved Zack's life. (implied main idea)

INTERPRETING DETAILS

Some questions on the PLAN Reading Test could require you to make simple **inferences about how details are used** in a passage. As you have seen so far in this chapter, the primary purpose of details is to support the main idea. When asked about a particular detail, what you must do is analyze how the detail supports the main idea (or how it does not).

You also need to be prepared to **interpret minor or subtly stated details** in a passage. These details may appear in the middle of other information, but they are important to look for. The author might present a fact or mention a seemingly random detail when describing a person or setting or so on. Although the particular detail may not be crucial to supporting the overall main idea, you, as the reader, could still be asked to recognize it and interpret its purpose or meaning (explain the author's intent in including it) as it relates to the text as a whole.

32

Read the passage below. After reading it, study the questions and statements that follow it. They refer to its main idea and the details that support it, even though they might be minor or subtly stated details.

> Robert tried to read his newspaper, but his attention kept straying. The early morning rain was lighter now, but just a bit. The sound of a slow drizzle could still be heard hitting the canopy that poorly sheltered him. Robert peered anxiously down a street in the predawn darkness. Maybe she wasn't coming.

1. What is the main idea of the passage above?

Robert is waiting in an early morning rain for someone he is anxious about seeing.

2. Which details directly support the main idea?

The early morning rain is lighter but still falling in a drizzle. (clearly stated)

Robert is peering anxiously down a street in the predawn darkness. (clearly stated)

3. In what way can a reader interpret the details?

Robert is not totally confident that the person whom he is there to meet is coming. This is not clearly stated, but it is implied by the fact that the author combines the description of Robert peering anxiously with the last sentence: "Maybe she wasn't coming."

4. How does the author use the subtle detail of Robert trying to read a newspaper?

Trying to read but not being able to do so is often associated with a person being distracted and unable to concentrate. The fact that Robert cannot focus on the newspaper he is trying to read adds to the mood that there is something important or intense about his pending meeting.

RECOGNIZING DETAILS THAT SUPPORT A SPECIFIC POINT

Some questions concerning more complicated passages could ask you to **recognize how details from different sections of a passage support a point**. This might mean choosing the detail (in the answer choices) that best communicates something you understood from the passage. It might also involve tying together details from throughout a passage to get a picture of a person, place, or event.

Understanding the Main Idea, Supporting Details, and Author's Approach

Look at this example.

Geronimo

Geronimo is the most famous of the Apaches. He and his small band of warriors, plus twelve women and six children, managed to resist five thousand United States soldiers and perhaps three thousand Mexican soldiers from 1881–1886.

He was a talker—not an orator of eloquence but a spokesman, a debater, a thrasher-
5 out of ideas. With either revolver or rifle, he was one of the best Chiricahua marksmen.

What made Geronimo such a remarkable leader? His fearlessness in battle, his apparent ability to foretell future events, and his sharp intelligence all gave his advice deep authority. In addition, his refusal to give in when faced with hopeless odds inspired others.

By his family he was named Goyahkla, which is usually taken to mean "one who
10 yawns." It was the Mexicans who started calling him Geronimo, perhaps for St. Jerome. The name came from a battle in which Goyahkla repeatedly ran through a hail of bullets to kill soldiers with his knife. When they saw the Apache warrior coming toward them, they began to yell out in desperation, "Geronimo!"

1. Which of the following is a reason the author gives for supporting his claim that Geronimo was a great leader?

   A. His refusal to give up
   B. His ability to defeat Mexicans in battle
   C. The fact he was a talker
   D. The fact that he had great marksmanship

Answer A is correct. When discussing what made Geronimo a remarkable leader, the author points out that his "refusal to give in when faced with hopeless odds inspired others." This implies that Geronimo's refusal to give up made him a great leader.

While the author does state that Geronimo fought in battles, he does not mention victories over Mexicans as one of the attributes for Geronimo being a great leader. (Answer B is eliminated.) While the author does state that Geronimo was a "talker," the author does not claim that this helped to make him a great leader. (Answer C is eliminated.) While the author does mention that Geronimo was a great marksman, this fact does not support the notion that Geronimo was a great leader. (Answer D is eliminated.)

Chapter 2

2. In the passage, the word *Apache* refers to:

   A. Mexicans who named Goyahkla "Geronimo."

   B. a group of Chiricahua marksmen.

   C. a Native American term meaning "one who yawns."

   D. Native Americans led by Geronimo.

Answer D is correct. A close reading of the passage reveals that the Apaches were a tribe of warriors, women, and children led by Geronimo.

In the passage, no specific name is given to Mexicans who named Goyahkla "Geronimo." (Answer A is eliminated.) The author refers to Geronimo, not the Apache people, as a Chiricahua marksman. (Answer B is eliminated.) The passage reveals that the term *Goyahkla* means "one who yawns." (Answer C is eliminated.)

3. Which of the following facts can you infer from the passage?

   A. Geronimo won many followers because people respected him.

   B. Geronimo was believed to be a saint by those who followed him.

   C. Geronimo was often cautious in battle.

   D. Geronimo's favorite weapon was the revolver.

Answer A is correct. The author states that Geronimo's fearlessness, ability to foretell future events, and sharp intelligence all gave his advice deep authority, and his refusal to give in inspired others. These details together allow readers to infer that people followed Geronimo because they respected him.

The passage says that the name "Geronimo" may have been derived from St. Jerome and that it was given to him by the Mexicans, not the Native Americans who followed Geronimo. (Answer B is eliminated.) The passage describes Geronimo as fearlessly charging into battle, even running through a hail of bullets while armed with only a knife. This does not lead readers to infer he was cautious in battle. (Answer C is eliminated.) Although the passage does state that Geronimo was a good marksman with a revolver, it also states that he was a good marksman with a rifle and describes him, on one occasion, charging into battle with just his knife. Readers cannot infer that the revolver was Geronimo's favorite weapon from the passage. (Answer D is eliminated.)

Understanding the Main Idea, Supporting Details, and Author's Approach

Practice 3: Supporting Details

Below are two passages. Both contain details that support a main idea. See if you can correctly answer the questions after each passage.

During the early 1900s, Hollywood and New Jersey were competitors for the movie industry. New Jersey was desirable because so many actors and actresses worked on Broadway, which is near New
5 Jersey. However, outdoor scenes required lots of natural light. As a result, Hollywood, nestled in the hills of sunny southern California, became the better choice for year-round filming. By 1911, fifteen film companies had made their home there.

1. Which of the following statements best expresses the author's main idea?

    A. Hollywood is located in California while New Jersey is closer to Broadway.

    B. Hollywood became the home of the movie industry largely for geographical reasons.

    C. Hollywood, California, is naturally a much sunnier environment than New Jersey.

    D. Most early actors got their start in Broadway and only later became movie stars.

2. When did Hollywood become the home of the motion-picture industry?

    A. Before 1900

    B. After 1911

    C. Between 1900 and 1911

    D. In the year 1911

3. Which of the following is a reason the author gives for why Hollywood was a better choice for making movies?

    A. Hollywood is warmer than New Jersey.

    B. Hollywood is farther from Broadway than New Jersey.

    C. Hollywood has more natural light than New Jersey.

    D. Hollywood has more attractive outdoor scenery than New Jersey.

Chapter 2

Excerpt from "Truthfulness"

by Charles Dudley Warner

Truthfulness is as essential in literature as it is in conduct, in fiction as it is in the report of an actual occurrence. Falsehood vitiates a poem, a painting, exactly as it does a life. Truthfulness is a quality like simplicity. Simplicity in literature is mainly a matter of clear vision and lucid expression, however complex the subject-matter may be; exactly as in life,
5 simplicity does not so much depend upon external conditions as upon the spirit in which one lives. It may be more difficult to maintain simplicity of living with a great fortune than in poverty, but simplicity of spirit—that is, superiority of soul to circumstance—is possible in any condition. Unfortunately the common expression that a certain person has wealth is not so true as it would be to say that wealth has him. The life of one with great possessions
10 and corresponding responsibilities may be full of complexity; the subject of literary art may be exceedingly complex; but we do not set complexity over against simplicity. For simplicity is a quality essential to true life as it is to literature of the first class; it is opposed to parade, to artificiality, to obscurity.

4. Which of the following points would the author most likely agree with?

A. Truthfulness must transcend circumstances.

B. A truthful person is one who lives a simple life.

C. A materially successful person cannot attain inner simplicity.

D. Most kinds of literature bear little resemblance to reality.

RECOGNIZING THE FUNCTION OF A PART OF A PASSAGE

At times, a question on the PLAN Reading Test might ask you to identify the **clear function of a part of a passage**. You will need to determine what role that particular portion of a text plays. As you read earlier in the section about details, this might mean you must find a phrase or sentence that serves to support an idea, add to an inference, or clarify a point. The question might refer to a larger section of text, such as a paragraph. Consider whether the part of the passage acts as one of the following:

Function	Description
Introduction	The **introduction** appears at the beginning of the passage. It contains a topic sentence, usually introduces the central idea, and sets up the remainder of the passage.
Supporting Detail	**Supporting details** elaborate on and help readers understand the main idea. Details also help set the scene of a passage (often the case in literary prose).
Topic Sentence	A **topic sentence** usually appears near the beginning of the passage. It states or implies the main idea of the passage.
Transitional Element	A **transitional element** is a phrase or sentence that helps the passage shift fluently from one point or idea to another.
Conclusion	The **conclusion** is a portion of text (often a paragraph or a closing sentence) at the end of the passage that summarizes the passage and brings it to a close.

Understanding the Main Idea, Supporting Details, and Author's Approach

Practice 4: Recognizing the Function of a Part of a Passage

Read the passage below. Then answer the questions that follow, which deal with recognizing the function of a part of a passage.

Hannah Farnham Sawyer Lee

In the early nineteenth century, the United States stood as a beacon of liberty among the nations of the world. But from the perspective of the women living in that time, not much had changed. In this atmosphere of limitation and strict gender roles, the writing of Hannah Farnham Sawyer Lee is particularly noteworthy. The twenty-plus books she wrote
5   cast light on this little-known period in women's literature.

Hannah Lee, a doctor's daughter, found herself a widow left with three little girls to bring up alone. At the age of fifty, she turned to writing to make a living and support her family. Between 1837 and 1854, Lee penned around two dozen novels, short-story collections, and essays. Most of her work focused on the struggles of women facing
10   financial, social, and personal difficulties.

Her characters were as gritty and determined as she was. For example, Lee's novel *Grace Seymour*, written in 1830, detailed the tribulations of the title character during the Revolutionary War. In a harsh atmosphere of deprivation and dread, Grace contends with crushing poverty, her growing sense of patriotism, and ongoing conflicts with her Tory
15   father. Grace's story concludes with her happy wedding to an officer in the American army.

Lee also added to other literary works of the day. *The Memoir of Hannah Adams* by Joseph Tuckerman had been a popular book, and Lee wrote a sequel using his character. The fictional Hannah Adams was much like Hannah Lee the writer, and in this character the author found her true voice. Reflecting her own reality, Lee's version of Hannah was
20   an upright model of virtue and wisdom who rises above her difficulties to become a writer herself.

In her writings, which often did not include the author's name, Lee used this formula time and again. Her writing style and novel characterization of women often were the only distinctive clues that a certain work had come from the pen of Hannah Sawyer Lee. Lee
25   had no leanings toward what was later defined as "feminism"—she in fact disapproved of the idea of the superiority of women. Still, her characters arguably fit the feminist profile. In a time when women were expected to be delicate, wilting flowers, Lee's women are staunch, forceful, independent, and determined to make their lives better through their own efforts.

30   Though Lee was basically an average writer, she occupies a prominent place in history for her groundbreaking ideas and her unusual heroines. But despite her literary accomplishments, Hannah Sawyer Lee's name has faded from the pantheon of America's notable authors, leaving only a fascinating footnote.

Chapter 2

1. The fact that Hannah Farnham Sawyer Lee published over twenty novels serves as:

    A. a part of the introduction of the passage.

    B. a transitional phrase in the passage.

    C. a detail meant to show Lee was a major writer.

    D. a conclusion to the author's main idea.

2. What function do the author's descriptions of Lee's main characters play in the passage?

    A. They serve as introductions to the passage.

    B. They serve as conclusions to the passage.

    C. They form the main idea of the passage.

    D. They serve as details supporting an idea.

Understanding the Main Idea, Supporting Details, and Author's Approach

AUTHOR'S APPROACH

Some questions on the PLAN Reading Test will ask you to recognize different characteristics of an author's approach. The **author's approach** refers to the manner in which an author chooses to convey a message.

Several key elements comprise an author's approach. Below are some elements you could be required to recognize to correctly answer questions on the PLAN.

Element	Description
Genre	The **genre** an author uses helps define his or her approach. Does the author choose to tell a story through literary prose? Is it a fiction or nonfiction piece? Is the author's text an essay meant to inform or make an argument? The choice of genre is one indication an author gives readers about how a text is meant to be read and perceived.
Structure	The **structure** of a written work refers to how it is organized. Some passages may have titles and subtitles. Informational passages often have headings and subheadings. Many passages share a similar structure: an introduction that states or implies the main idea, a body consisting of supporting details, and a conclusion that wraps up the passage and restates the main idea. Literary prose may be structured as a narrative, a memoir, an essay, and so on.
Kinds of Evidence	Some authors use certain **kinds of evidence** to support main ideas or to argue points. Some may use facts, data, information, expert opinions, comparisons and contrasts, or historical evidence and examples. Others might refer to details such as the way a person acts, the state of the weather, or the overall mood. The reader must discern whether the evidence is appropriate and relevant to effectively support the author's ideas.
Point of View	The **author's point of view** is an important element of his or her approach. The author's point of view refers to the perspective from which he or she chooses to tell a story. The point of view in a piece could be first person, second person, or third person.

Features of Point of View	
First Person	The narrator tells the story from his own point of view, saying "I did this" or "I did that." Perhaps the most famous example of recent times is J. D. Salinger's *The Catcher in the Rye*.
Second Person	The book itself addresses the reader, as if the reader is an active character in the book. For example, "You are walking down the street one morning when…" Second person narration is rarely used. Jay McInerney's *Bright Lights, Big City*, is one of only a few examples of second person narration.
Third Person	This point of view contains the majority of fiction written before the 20th century. In third person, a narrator moves unseen among the characters, relating their actions. There are two kinds of third person narration, with different advantages and difficulties:
omniscient	Narrators can see everything and everywhere, even relating the characters' thoughts. Charles Dickens's *Oliver Twist* is an example of omniscient third.
limited	Third person narration (sometimes called **approximate third**) centers on one character and observes only what he sees, hears, feels or does. It will also sometimes include his thoughts. Erich Maria Remarque's *All Quiet on the Western Front*, as it focuses on the soldier Baumer, is an example of this kind of work.

AUTHOR'S CLEAR INTENT

Some PLAN questions could require you to recognize the **clear intent of the author or narrator**. In other words, what is the author's purpose in writing the text? Or, what is the narrator's purpose in a passage? Identifying the main idea of the passage and the kinds of supporting details the author uses will point you toward its overall intent.

Some authors write to persuade others to agree with them, while others simply want to inform or educate.

You can determine the clear intent of the author from the way he writes. For example, imagine that one reporter writes a news article about water-conservation laws. Another reporter writes an opinion-based article to persuade others to conserve water. The first reporter aims to inform, while the second reporter is motivated to persuade others to agree with his personal beliefs about water conservation.

Understanding the Main Idea, Supporting Details, and Author's Approach

Author's Purpose		
Purpose	**Definition**	**Sample Titles**
to inform	to present facts and details	"Ocean Fishes"
to entertain	to amuse or offer enjoyment	"Time I Slipped in the Mud"
to persuade	to urge action on an issue	"Raise Penalties for Polluters"
to instruct	to teach concepts and facts	"Tips for Healthy Living"
to create suspense	to convey uncertainty	"Will Tom Win the Race?"
to motivate	to encourage to act	"You Can Survive"
to cause doubt	to be skeptical	"Are Adults Responsible?"
to describe an event	to narrate	"9-11: USA Under Fire!"
to teach a lesson	to furnish knowledge	"Mastering Exponents"
to introduce a character	to describe a person's traits	"First Look at Captain Nemo"
to create a mood	to establish atmosphere	"Gloom in the House of Usher"
to relate an adventure	to tell an exciting story	"Lost in a Cave"
to share a personal experience	to tell about an event in your life	"The Time I Learned to Share"
to describe feelings	to communicate emotions through words	"When My Dog Died"

Chapter 2

Practice 5: Author's Approach

Read the passage below, and then answer the questions that follow regarding the author's approach.

    In the Catskills I found something I'd missed after four decades of living in cities: simple courtesy. Like a friendly wave, for example. It is unthinkable not to return one…Walt Meade, a naturalist who lives in Roxbury, on the Catskill's northern slope, says, "I was going to Grand Gorge when Jane Hubble drove by and waved. But I didn't see her
5 till it was too late. The next time I saw her, she berated me, 'I wasted a perfectly good wave on you, Walt Meade. And I don't know if I'm going to wave at you again.'" Time after time, stories of compassion come out of the Catskills. "When my dad's barn burned down, the neighbors put a new one up in three days." "When our daughter was killed, the neighbors just came in and took over." The genuineness of the Catskills calls out like a
10 distant memory.

                                                                                – editorial in *The Wilson Gazette*

1. The author strives to achieve his purpose by:

    A. narrating from a first-person point of view.

    B. contrasting examples of life in the city and life in the Catskills.

    C. including anecdotal examples that support his claim.

    D. telling a fictional story.

2. Jane Hubble's wave and her berating of Walt Meade serve as:

    A. the author's point of view.

    B. examples supporting the author's point about the Catskills.

    C. details of the author's personal experiences in the Catskills.

    D. elements of structure in the passage.

3. In the passage, the phrase "distant memory" best implies which of the following?

    A. Courtesy used to be more common than it is today.

    B. People are more genuine in the Catskills than in other places.

    C. The author cannot remember ever visiting a place as genuine as the Catskills.

    D. Many people have forgotten how to be courteous.

Understanding the Main Idea, Supporting Details, and Author's Approach

CHAPTER 2 SUMMARY

Below are key concepts covered in chapter 2 and some of the reading comprehension skills you must be prepared to demonstrate on the PLAN Reading Test.

Identify or infer the main idea of a passage.

Locate supporting details.

Make simple inferences about how details are used in a passage.

Locate basic facts stated in a passage.

Summarize basic events and ideas.

Interpret minor or subtly stated details in a passage.

Discern which details in a certain passage support a given point.

Use details from different sections of a complex informational passage to support a specific point or argument.

Recognize the clear function of a part of a passage.

Understand the author's approach in writing the passage.

Determine and understand the clear intent of an author or a narrator in a passage.

CHAPTER 2 REVIEW: MAIN IDEA, SUPPORTING DETAILS, AND AUTHOR'S APPROACH

Below are two passages. The questions that follow them will allow you to practice the skills covered in this chapter.

PROSE FICTION: This passage is an excerpt from Hannah Sawyer Lee's *Rich Enough: A Tale of the Times* (©1837 Whipple & Damrell)

The spring had returned with its new-born beauty, its swelling buds, its tender grass; here and there a tree in the city anticipated the season of leaves, and put forth its verdant honors. "Now, ma'am," said Lucy, who had long been a faithful domestic in the family, "if you are going particular, and don't expose yourself by going into the garden, and will take the cough-drops regularly, morning and evening, you will get rid of your cold. This is just the season when everybody gets well that got sick as you did."

"How was that?" said Mrs. Draper.

"Why, when the sap was going down the trees in the autumn; but now it is going up."

But whether the sap had already gone up, or for some other reason, which was as clear to human perception, Frances did not shake off her wearing cough. Mr. Draper was not alarmed at it; it was very unobtruding, and he had become *used to it*. It was not one of those vulgar, hoarse coughs, that, till we connect danger with it, often excites indignation in those who are listening to an interesting narrative, or to a reader, who is obliged to wait till the impertinent paroxysm is over. Mrs. Draper's was quite a lady-like cough, low and gentle, and seemed rather like impeded respiration.

Visitors would sometimes observe, when they went away, "Mrs. Draper is still a handsome woman, though she has lost her bloom. What a pity she has that affected little cough! it really spoils her; it is nothing but a habit; she could easily break herself of it, if anybody would be honest enough to tell her." This task rested with Lucy alone; but it was all in vain. Frances took the cough-drops morning and evening, and still the disagreeable habit remained. Mr. Draper was very little at home; and when he was, his mind was engaged by new projects. Anxiety, however, did not rob him of sleep: he was too successful; he seemed to have the Midas-like art of turning everything to gold:—his thousands were rapidly accumulating, and half a million was now the point at which he determined to stop. Mrs. Draper's slight cough did not attract his attention; but if her appetite failed, he grew anxious, and feared she was not well.

Week after week passed, and still it was impossible for Mr. Draper to leave the city. At length, a letter arrived from Charlotte, claiming the visit; and he substituted one of his clerks to conduct his family to his brother's residence. Here, though not more than forty miles from the city, Mrs. Draper found the freshness and novelty of country life. The family were farmers, children and all. Charlotte was acquainted with all the little details belonging to a farm, and took as much interest as her husband did in the growth of grain, the raising of pigs and poultry, and feeding cattle in the best and most economical

Understanding the Main Idea, Supporting Details, and Author's Approach

manner. She displayed her dairy with its cheese arranged on shelves, her white pans of milk, and her newly-churned butter, which impregnated the
80 air with its sweetness.

1. Mr. Draper did not seem to notice Mrs. Draper's cough because:

   A. it was rare and ever-lessening.

   B. it was not a loud or violent cough.

   C. it was something he had learned to live with.

   D. he was too enamored with country life.

2. Which of the following best describes Mr. Draper's attitude as depicted in the passage?

   F. He is deeply in love with his wife.

   G. He struggles to make his business successful.

   H. He obsesses over his wife's health.

   J. He is consumed with accumulating wealth.

3. What task does Mr. Draper give one of his clerks rather than assuming himself?

   A. attending to Mrs. Draper's illness

   B. accompanying his family to the country

   C. overseeing his business affairs

   D. providing Mrs. Draper with medicine

4. The passage implies that Mrs. Draper's husband is:

   F. deeply concerned for her well-being.

   G. not fond of his brother's family.

   H. stressed and worried about his failing business.

   J. too busy to notice her failing health.

5. The ineffectiveness of the cough drops suggests that:

   A. Lucy does not give Mrs. Draper the right medicine.

   B. Mrs. Draper's cough is simply a habit.

   C. Mrs. Draper's illness is more serious than anyone realizes.

   D. Mr. Draper should not be so anxious about his wife.

6. The statement, "Here, though not more than forty miles from the city, Mrs. Draper found the freshness and novelty of country life" (lines 66–68), implies that Mrs. Draper:

   F. enjoys her time in the country.

   G. does not like having to go to the country.

   H. feels out of place on a farm.

   J. gets healthy while living on a farm.

7. The passage suggests that Lucy:

   A. resents working for Mrs. Draper.

   B. is not trusted by Mr. Draper.

   C. sincerely cares for Mrs. Draper.

   D. believes Mrs. Draper's cough is merely habit.

Chapter 2

SOCIAL SCIENCES: A Historical Account of Hoover Dam.

In 1905, floodwaters spilled over the banks of the Colorado River in the Southwest United States. In 1916, another major flood swept the Yuma
5   Valley, wiping out thousands of acres of fertile farmlands. Something needed to be done to control the raging river. As a result of this need, one of the most significant technological marvels of the
10 twentieth century, Hoover Dam, now stands near the southern tip of Nevada.

The man who first proposed the dam project was Arthur Powell Davis of the Reclamation Service. Powell was a
15 civil engineer who specialized in the building of dams and canals. Believing that the canyons of southern Nevada had the potential to support a dam, he studied the area diligently for twenty
20 years, working out problems of logistics and topography. The original site proposed for the dam was in Boulder Canyon, but Davis discovered that a geological fault line crossed the
25 area, making a dam a risky venture. He looked elsewhere, finally settling on Black Canyon.

At the time construction began, the Hoover Dam project was the most
30 monumental undertaking in the history of the world. Although such a feat had never been attempted before, the contractors planned to complete construction within seven years. The
35 first part of their plan was to blast and drill out four fifty-foot tunnels alongside the site to divert the raging river so the dam's foundation could be laid. Then the building of the dam itself
40 could proceed while the riverbed was dry.

As a result of the Great Depression, thousands of desperate unemployed men poured into southern Nevada
45 looking for steady work on the dam project. They found jobs—but at a price. The work carried incredible risks. It was hellishly hot in the canyon. At times the temperature climbed to
50 120 degrees. In the tunnels, the temperature often hit 140 degrees, and carbon monoxide poisoning was a constant threat. By August, fourteen men had died of heat prostration and
55 sunstroke alone. And always there was the danger of accidental death or dismemberment from falling rock or explosions. Still, at times the payroll swelled to some 5000 workers; a whole
60 town, Boulder City, had to be built nearby to accommodate these men and their families.

The work went on as relentlessly as the sweltering sun; three shifts ran
65 around the clock, twenty-four hours a day, seven days a week, with only two days off per year—Christmas and the Fourth of July. Two years of hard, intense labor were needed just to
70 prepare the site for the dam; after ten million cubic yards of rock were removed, building the immense structure itself began. By the time the project was finished, enough concrete
75 had been used to have built a sixteen-foot-wide roadway from Manhattan to San Francisco.

At a dizzying pace, the awesome concrete face of the dam rose higher
80 and higher, until it topped out at sixty stories tall. Finally the finishing touches were laid in place—and on May 29, 1935, the colossal dam was completed, two years ahead of
85 schedule. The Colorado River was

Understanding the Main Idea, Supporting Details, and Author's Approach

diverted back where it belonged, and Lake Mead began to fill behind the wall of the dam. The fearsome Colorado was at last tamed.

90 For Depression-era Americans, this monumental structure became a symbol of hope for a country in economic turmoil. The name "Hoover Dam" was adopted in 1947 to honor
95 Herbert Hoover, the standing president at the time of the scheme's beginning. So it is known to this day.

8. The purpose of this passage is to:
   F. argue that the Colorado River could not have been tamed without a dam.
   G. help readers understand why dams are needed in places like Nevada.
   H. educate readers regarding the history of the construction of the Hoover Dam.
   J. help readers understand historically how the Hoover Dam impacted the Great Depression.

9. The dam was named for:
   A. the president serving at the time of its completion.
   B. the president serving at the time the project began.
   C. the engineer who first proposed the project.
   D. the man who chose the location for the dam.

10. The fact that the dam rose at a "dizzying pace" suggest that the construction crews:
    F. encountered a lot of problems building the dam.
    G. had trouble working in the intense heat of the desert.
    H. worked slower than had originally been expected.
    J. worked at an incredibly rapid rate.

11. Which statement from the passage best supports the notion that the Hoover Dam was an ambitious undertaking?
    A. The Hoover Dam project was the most monumental undertaking in the history of the world.
    B. Thousands of desperate unemployed men poured into southern Nevada looking for steady work on the dam project.
    C. The Colorado River was diverted back where it belonged, and Lake Mead began to fill behind the wall of the dam.
    D. On May 29, 1935, the colossal dam was completed, two years ahead of schedule.

12. According to the passage, the site of Hoover Dam was chosen mainly because:

    F. it was an extremely warm area.

    G. the land's natural formations made dam construction very easy.

    H. a fault line existed in the area, making it well suited for construction.

    J. the canyon walls there could support a large structure like a dam.

Understanding the Main Idea, Supporting Details, and Author's Approach

Chapter 3
Reading for Relationships: Sequential Order, Connections, and Cause-Effect

Some questions on the PLAN Reading Test will require you to be able to **determine sequential order** within a passage. Others will require you to make connections and **identify clear relationships between people, ideas, and so on**. Still others will require you to **identify clear, subtly stated, or implied cause-effect relationships**. These questions, ranging from recognition of relationships in uncomplicated passages to understanding relationship dynamics in more challenging passages, earn the following points.

13–15	Determine when (e.g., first, last, before, after) or if an event occurred in uncomplicated passages
	Recognize clear cause-effect relationships described within a single sentence in a passage
16–19	Identify relationships between main characters in uncomplicated literary narratives
	Recognize clear cause-effect relationships within a single paragraph in uncomplicated literary narratives
20–23	Order simple sequences of events in uncomplicated literary narratives
	Identify clear relationships between people, ideas, and so on in uncomplicated passages
	Identify clear cause-effect relationships in uncomplicated passages
24–27	Order sequences of events in uncomplicated passages
	Understand relationships between people, ideas, and so on in uncomplicated passages
	Identify clear relationships between characters, ideas, and so on in more challenging literary narratives
	Understand implied or subtly stated cause-effect relationships in uncomplicated passages
	Identify clear cause-effect relationships in more challenging passages
28–32	Order sequences of events in more challenging passages
	Understand the dynamics between people, ideas, and so on in more challenging passages
	Understand implied or subtly stated cause-effect relationships in more challenging passages

Reading for Relationships: Sequential Order, Connections, and Cause-Effect

In this chapter, you will review how to apply your reading skills to determine sequential order, make connections, and identify cause-effect relationships in both uncomplicated and more challenging passages.

SEQUENTIAL ORDER

Sequence refers to the order in which events happen. When writers use **sequence of events**, they arrange the details of a story in the order in which they happened. This is also called time order or chronological order. Sequence of events can go from the first to the last event or from the last to the first event. Usually, stories will be arranged from the first to the last event. Think of the last time friends told you a personal story. Did they use time order? Did they tell the story from the first to the last event or the other way around? Below are some transitional words and phrases that are often used to show a sequence of events.

Sequence of Events Transitions		
after	finally	then
at last	first	thereafter
at once	meanwhile	when
eventually	next	

Some questions on the PLAN Reading Test could require you to determine the sequence of events in a passage. To practice this skill, read the passage below. Then answer the question that follows.

Harry Houdini

In the summer of 1912, a man was chained and then nailed into a wooden box. The box was bound with rope and steel cables and lowered into the East River. Minutes passed as the audience waited to see what would happen. Fearing for the man's life, many gasped for breath themselves. Suddenly, the man emerged from the water, unharmed and freed
5 from his chains. His name was Harry Houdini.

1. Which of the following occurred before a box was lowered into the East River?

   A. People gasped for breath.

   B. A man emerged from the water unharmed.

   C. A man was chained.

   D. People feared for a man's life.

The correct answer is C. A close reading of the passage reveals the sequence of events. Of the four possible answers, only the man being chained occurred prior to a box being lowered into the East River.

Chapter 3

Practice 1: Sequential Order

Read the two passages that follow. Then answer the questions about sequence.

PROSE FICTION: This passage is an excerpt from Roland Alaway's novel *Conway Finch* (Rameses Publishing ©2012).

"Conway Finch!" The tone in Ms. Bagwell's voice made it clear that she was not at all amused. Suddenly, a garden snake in the teacher's desk drawer did not seem quite so humorous. "Conway Finch, if there were any doubt before, you've most certainly erased it. You are bad! Do you hear me? Bad, bad, bad! That's what you are—bad to the core!"

5   Inwardly, Conway rolled his eyes. This certainly wasn't the first time he'd heard this speech. Over Ms. Bagwell's shoulder, the rambunctious fifth grader could see Hillary peering through the glass door window.

"Are you paying attention to me, young man? You had better start getting your act together. I'm sick and tired of Ms. Watersby constantly sending you to my office. If it isn't
10 a fish in her purse, it's shoe polish on her glasses. Why must you insist on getting your jollies off of torturing a woman who is attempting to do nothing more than give you an education?"

Conway continued sitting there, pretending to listen. As he saw it, there was no reason to speak—no sense trying to defend or explain himself. The grownups didn't care anyway.
15 They'd already declared him "bad," so he figured he might as well have fun meeting their expectations. He hoped Ms. Bagwell would hurry up and finish. He just wanted her to pronounce her judgment. Which one would it be this time? Calling his father, who would surely whup him once he got home? Make him report to Ms. Watersby's classroom every day after school for a month to clean erasers and write sentences like "I will not put a snake
20 in my teacher's desk, blah, blah, blah"? No matter. He'd done 'em all before. He'd do any of 'em again.

"Well, this is the last straw, Mr. Finch. No more playing around. I am going to break you of this rebellious, defiant hooliganism once and for all."

Just then the door behind Conway opened. Ms. Bagwell looked toward the entering
25 figure and smiled. Conway turned to see an intimidating stranger. He was dressed in black from head to foot, a scar and eyepatch decorating the right side of his face.

"You must be Conway Finch, eh, lad?" growled the looming visitor. "It looks like you and me is going to become well acquainted."

1. Which of the following events occurs first?

   A. Conway puts a snake in his teacher's desk.

   B. Ms. Bagwell tells Conway he is "bad."

   C. Conway puts shoe polish on his teacher's glasses.

   D. An intimidating figure enters Ms. Bagwell's office.

Reading for Relationships: Sequential Order, Connections, and Cause-Effect

2. What does Conway do after Ms. Bagwell tells him she's going to break him of his rebellious, defiant behavior?

   A. He rolls his eyes.

   B. He turns to see an intimidating stranger.

   C. He pretends to listen to her lecture.

   D. He sees Hillary through the window.

Chick-fil-A

Founded by S. Truett Cathy, the first Chick-fil-A restaurant opened in Atlanta in 1967. It grew out of Cathy's original restaurant, the Dwarf Grill, and his innovative way of preparing chicken to be served as a sandwich. Currently, Chick-fil-A operates
5 more than sixteen hundred restaurants in forty states. By 2011, it reported over $4.1 billion in profits, making it one of the nation's most prosperous restaurant chains. This feat is remarkable, considering that Cathy, a devout Christian, insists that his restaurants remain closed on Sundays.

S. Truett Cathy

3. Which event occurred before 1967?

   A. Chick-fil-A opened its first restaurant in Atlanta.

   B. S. Truett Cathy owned a restaurant called the Dwarf Grill.

   C. Chick-fil-A operated more than sixteen hundred restaurants.

   D. Cathy's restaurants were present in forty states.

4. Which of the following occurred last?

   A. S. Truett Cathy became a devout Christian.

   B. S. Truett Cathy insisted that his restaurants remain closed on Sundays.

   C. S. Truett Cathy developed an innovative new way to serve chicken.

   D. Chick-fil-A reported over $4.1 billion in profits.

Chapter 3

RELATIONSHIPS BETWEEN PEOPLE, CHARACTERS, IDEAS, AND EVENTS

Some questions might require you to **identify relationships between people, ideas, and so on**. For example, you might be asked to determine how one character in a story feels about another character or a situation. You might be asked to recognize the connection between an individual mentioned in a passage and a particular circumstance or idea. Or you might need to recognize how two events, ideas, or circumstances in a passage are connected.

Read the passage below, and review the analysis that follows.

> Evelyn said nothing. Occasionally glancing politely at her uninvited dinner guest, she anxiously waited for him to finish his boring tale so that she could return her full attention to the passing snow-covered mountains outside the dining car window.

How would you describe Evelyn's relationship to her dinner guest? Are they close friends? Are they involved in a romantic relationship? No, obviously not. The narrator refers to the guest as an "uninvited dinner guest" and says that Evelyn finds him boring and can't wait for him to stop talking so she can enjoy looking out her window. These facts suggest to the reader that Evelyn does not care for her dinner guest's company and wishes he would be quiet, if not leave.

Some questions might require you to demonstrate that you **understand the dynamics between people, ideas, and so on**. Dynamics encompass relationships and include all of the forces that influence them.

Read the passage below, and review the analysis that follows.

> "So much for this weekend!" Chip angrily mumbled. There was no pleasing Murphy. No matter how sharp the proposal, Murphy would not be satisfied until he had thrown in his two cents and ordered half of it reworked. If Chip could have afforded to tell Murphy to go jump off a bridge he would have, but he knew he couldn't do that.

Based on the passage above, what dynamics would you say exist between Chip and Murphy? Are they friends? Is one a teacher and the other a student? Are they neighbors? The passage doesn't tell you directly. But you can infer from the available information that Murphy holds some position of authority over Chip that Chip must respect. Perhaps Murphy is Chip's boss. Maybe he is a client paying for some service that Chip offers, and Chip must satisfy him in order to get paid. The narrator tells you that Chip cannot afford to walk away from what Murphy pays him, no matter how much he might dislike working for him.

COMPARISON AND CONTRAST

Writers also use comparison and contrast to organize ideas. **Comparison** highlights similarities or measures people, circumstances, ideas, and so on against one another. **Contrast** highlights differences.

Reading for Relationships: Sequential Order, Connections, and Cause-Effect

When writers compare and contrast ideas, they show how these ideas are both alike and different. For example, how would you compare and contrast skateboarding and bicycle riding? What about middle school and high school? Below are some transitions that are commonly used for comparison and contrast.

Comparing Ideas Transitions	
also	like
and	likewise
another	similarly
in addition	too

Contrasting Ideas Transitions	
but	on the other hand
however	unlike
in spite of	while
not	

For example, read the passage below, and review the analysis that follows.

> In some ways, water skiing and snow skiing are very similar. Both require the athlete to exhibit great balancing skills and to develop exceptional leg strength. However, the two sports have their obvious differences as well. When wanting to turn, a snow skier must put his weight on the opposite foot of the direction in which he wants to go, whereas a water skier puts the weight on the same foot.

The passage above compares and contrasts snow skiing and water skiing. When compared, both sports require athletes to have balancing skills and leg strength. However, the manner in which a skier turns is different in each sport.

CAUSE-EFFECT RELATIONSHIPS

Cause-effect relationships refer to how events in a passage relate to one another. A **cause** makes something happen. An **effect** is what happens due to the cause. What is the cause-effect relationship between good diet and health? What is the cause-effect relationship between poor study habits and poor grades? What other cause-effect relationships can you think of? Questions on the PLAN Reading Test might require you to recognize cause-effect relationships within a single sentence, a paragraph, or the passage as a whole. The following are transitional words and phrases that are often used to show cause and effect:

Chapter 3

Cause and Effect Transitions		
accordingly	due to	so
as a result	for example	so that is why
because	for that reason	therefore
consequently	hence	thus

Read the passage below, and review the analysis that follows.

> For years, psychologists and other mental health experts have claimed that people who commit violent crimes suffer from low self-esteem. However, the latest evidence now suggests that just the opposite is true. According to the latest research, most violent acts actually stem from perpetrators having an inflated sense of self-importance. They possess
> 5 extremely high, not low, self-esteem, and they react violently when their self-image is not validated or confirmed by others.

The passage above discusses a cause-effect relationship. According to the passage, the latest research reveals that high self-esteem is a trigger for many perpetrators of violent crimes. So in this passage, high self-esteem is a cause, and violent crime is an effect.

Sometimes, **cause-effect relationships might be implied or subtly stated** rather than clearly or directly stated. Read the passage below, and review the analysis that follows.

> Miriam wiped away the tear that slowly made its way down her cheek. Rarely did she weep anymore. Still, in quiet moments, when no one was there, she found herself thinking of her husband and wishing he were alive and still with her.

In the passage above, Miriam is sad. Although it is not directly stated, the reader can infer that Miriam's sadness stems from her husband's death. In this passage, then, Miriam's husband's death is a cause, and Miriam's emotion (her sadness) is an effect.

Reading for Relationships: Sequential Order, Connections, and Cause-Effect

Practice 2: Relationships between People, Characters, Ideas, and Events

Read the passages that follow. Then answer the questions dealing with relationships between people, characters, ideas, and events.

SOCIAL SCIENCES: This passage, "Interest Groups and Lobbyists," is taken from a high school social studies book (American Book Company ©2007).

Interest Groups and Lobbyists

Interest groups are different from political parties because, unlike parties that sponsor candidates and support a number of issues, interest groups tend to focus on a single issue and
5 seek to use the political process to either encourage or prevent change to existing policies. Since third parties rarely win elections in the United States, most interest groups choose to align themselves with one of the two major
10 parties rather than branching out on their own. This leads to interesting coalitions.

**Civil Rights Marchers
(Library of Congress)**

Coalitions are the banding together of different groups for the purpose of achieving political success. For instance, autoworkers in Michigan and civil rights activists in the South may, on the surface, not seem to have much in common. However, they may band
15 together for the purpose of supporting candidates that will back both their interests.

Some groups within a party might be seen as *radical* because they hold extreme opinions. For instance, those advocating massive government reforms and/or government control over certain institutions are often tagged as "radicals" (i.e., those
20 favoring government control of businesses or health care). Other groups are seen as *reactionary* because they "react" to what they view as radical changes or movements. Reactionary groups tend to value the status quo or want to see a return to more traditional ways. Since both groups tend to be seen as "too extreme" by
25 many citizens, they find it advantageous to be part of a larger coalition within one of the major parties.

Lobbying

To help get laws passed that are favorable to their cause, many interest groups hire lobbyists who work to influence legislation in Congress and/or state legislatures. Today, many corporations and special interest groups pay big money to
30 lobbyists who can influence Congress and state legislatures. Beginning in the 1980s, there has been increased concern about former elected officials turned lobbyists using their connections in Congress to win special consideration. In 2006, scandals surrounding lobbying practices on Capitol Hill led to the introduction of new legislation aimed at preventing corrupt deals between lobbyists and lawmakers.

Chapter 3

1. According to the article, how do interest groups differ from political parties?

    A. Interest groups support many political issues, while parties focus on just one.

    B. Interest groups do not lobby, but political parties often do.

    C. Interest groups focus on a cause, while parties focus on electing candidates.

    D. Interest groups do not engage in the political process, but parties do.

2. According to the passage, autoworkers in Michigan and civil rights activists in the South might band together if:

    A. they are able to lobby members of Congress first.

    B. working together proves to be mutually beneficial.

    C. members of each can effectively form an interest group.

    D. by doing so they can start a new political party.

3. According to the passage, if lobbying is an effect, which of the following is a cause?

    A. Political parties

    B. Political candidates

    C. Political causes

    D. Political scandals

HUMANITIES: This passage is an excerpt from an English textbook (American Book Company © 2008).

Hidden Dragon?

American films today are filled with spectacular fight scenes that are mixtures of dance, gymnastics, martial arts, and pure fantasy. The American interest in martial arts was first sparked by legendary martial arts master and actor, Bruce Lee. Lee was born in San Francisco in 1940, in the Year and the Hour of the Dragon. He practiced his particular
5 martial art so devotedly and had so much natural talent for it that he developed the art further than it had ever been developed before. He made several martial arts movies during the 1970s. The most famous of these movies—and some say his best one—is titled *Enter the Dragon*. In his movies, there was little of the special effects you see today. Lee himself performed most of the amazing moves seen in these movies.

10 Lee dedicated his life to practicing and teaching martial arts. In his movies, he always included not only thrilling fight scenes, but also dialogue in which his philosophy of martial arts is clarified. Lee's philosophy had little to do with unnecessary violence, and much to do with self-discipline and art. Lee died at a young age. To this day, his brilliant demonstrations of martial arts have never been surpassed in film.

Reading for Relationships: Sequential Order, Connections, and Cause-Effect

4. According to the passage, the American moviegoing public's modern fascination with martial arts fight scenes can be attributed to:

   A. today's martial arts films.

   B. the movie *Enter the Dragon*.

   C. a philosophy that emphasizes self-discipline.

   D. actor Bruce Lee.

5. According to the author, Lee would find the American public's fascination with excessive violence:

   A. contrary to his own views.

   B. consistent with martial arts.

   C. a natural consequence of martial arts.

   D. a cause of America's appreciation for his work.

CHAPTER 3 SUMMARY

Below are key concepts covered in chapter 3 and some of the reading comprehension skills you should be prepared to demonstrate on the PLAN Reading Test.

Determine when or if an event occurred in a passage.

Order sequences of events in uncomplicated and more challenging passages.

Identify comparisons and contrasts of people, characters, ideas, and so on.

Identify relationships between main characters in literary narratives.

Identify and understand relationships between people, ideas, and so on.

Understand the dynamics between people, ideas, and so on in a passage.

Recognize clear cause-effect relationships described within a single sentence, paragraph, or passage.

Identify implied or subtly stated cause-effect relationships in a passage.

CHAPTER 3 REVIEW

Below is a historical passage. The questions that follow will allow you to practice the skills covered in this chapter.

SOCIAL SCIENCES: The following passage is an adapted excerpt from a US history book (American Book Company ©2010).

Between 1917 and the beginning of World War II, Europe saw the rise of new forms of government. Russia pulled out of World War I in 1917 as a result of its
5   own revolution; the victorious Bolsheviks had established a communist government. Communism is a form of government in which the state owns nearly all property and controls the
10 nation's economy. Russia and a number of other nations became a new country under the communists: the Union of Soviet Socialist Republics (USSR), or Soviet Union.

15 In 1922, Joseph Stalin became the leader of the Soviet Union, a totalitarian state. A totalitarian state is one in which the government demands total loyalty from its people and controls every aspect
20 of society. Stalin ruled with an iron hand, executing his rivals and many of his own people to secure his position.

In 1933, Adolf Hitler became the leader of Germany. He led the Nazi Party
25 and established a totalitarian government as well. But the Nazis opposed the principle of communism. Under the Nazi regime, the government did not own all the property, but it did control the
30 economy and the ways in which private business owners conducted themselves.

Hitler knew that Germans were suffering in the aftermath of World War I. He blamed Germany's wartime
35 enemies and the German republican government for the country's woes. Hitler also relied on anti-Semitism (prejudice against Jewish people) to inflame the German people. European
40 Jews had long been objects of social discrimination. Ironically, Germany had a large Jewish population because that country had proved itself to be less anti-Semitic than France and many other
45 European nations years before. A number of Jewish citizens occupied positions of power in the republic and important financial posts in the falling economy. Those people proved to be
50 easy targets for those seeking to blame someone for Germany's plight. Using his powerful speaking abilities to rally Germans to his cause, Hitler employed nationalism and anti-Semitism to
55 establish himself as a totalitarian dictator and found his government, which he labeled the Third Reich.

In 1936, Hitler moved German troops into an area known as the Rhineland.
60 Such action directly violated the treaty that had ended WWI, and this invasion outraged a number of leaders. Fearing another war with Germany, the governments of Great Britain and France
65 did nothing. In March 1938, Hitler tested his boundaries again by annexing (claiming) Austria. Once again, he met no resistance. In September, he demanded the right to annex the
70 Sudetenland, the western region of Czechoslovakia in which 3.5 million ethnic Germans lived. Although few people wanted to admit it, Hitler's aggression was setting the stage for
75 another world war.

In an effort to avoid war, Great Britain and France signed a treaty with Hitler in which they agreed to overlook Hitler's capture of the Sudetenland in exchange
80 for his promise not to invade any more

Reading for Relationships: Sequential Order, Connections, and Cause-Effect

territories. (Such a policy is called *appeasement*, because it assumes that by giving aggressors what they want they will be satisfied enough to stop their
85 aggressive behavior.) One member of the British Parliament who fiercely opposed this approach was Winston Churchill. Churchill voiced his opposition, stating, "Britain and France had to choose
90 between war and dishonor. They chose dishonor; they will have war."

In 1939, Hitler broke his promise and invaded Poland. The following year, he invaded other countries in Western
95 Europe, including France. Then, in 1941, Hitler broke a nonaggression pact with Stalin and attacked the Soviet Union too. Adolf Hitler had led Europe into World War II.

1. According to the passage, when did Joseph Stalin become leader of the Soviet Union?

   A. Before Hitler ruled Germany
   B. After Great Britain and France signed a treaty in Munich
   C. During the height of World War II
   D. While German troops entered the Rhineland

2. Winston Churchill's quote implies that which of the following was a cause of World War II?

   F. Stalin's iron-handed rule
   G. Hitler's invasion of territories
   H. The policy of appeasement
   J. The advent of communism

3. Racist attitudes against Jewish people led to the:

   A. Russian Revolution.
   B. invasion of Austria.
   C. annexing of the Sudetenland.
   D. rise of the Nazis.

4. Which of the following events occurred first?

   F. Stalin's rise to power
   G. Hitler's rise to power
   H. Establishment of the Third Reich
   J. World War I

5. In what way was Stalin's government similar to Hitler's?

   A. Both governments' leaders were elected by the people.
   B. Both governments were ruled in a totalitarian fashion.
   C. Both governments had communist philosophies.
   D. Both governments wanted to expand their territory.

6. Churchill's attitude towards Hitler can best be described as:

   F. friendly.
   G. optimistic.
   H. untrusting.
   J. sympathetic.

7. The horrors of World War I led most directly to:

   A. Hitler's desire to rule Germany.

   B. Stalin's ability to gain power in the USSR.

   C. Churchill's endorsement of a treaty with Germany.

   D. Great Britain's willingness to engage in appeasement.

8. Many factors contributed to World War II. Which of the following events occurred last?

   F. Hitler's invasion of Poland

   G. Hitler's invasion of the Soviet Union

   H. Hitler's signing of a nonaggression pact

   J. Hitler's invasion of France

Reading for Relationships: Sequential Order, Connections, and Cause-Effect

Chapter 4
Interpreting Words and Phrases

Some questions on the PLAN Reading Test will require you to be able to **interpret the meanings of various words and phrases**. These questions earn points based on the following points, ranging from understanding implications of familiar language to determining meanings in more challenging passages.

13–15	Understand the implication of a familiar word or phrase and of simple descriptive language
16–19	Use context to understand basic figurative language
20–23	Use context to determine the appropriate meaning of some figurative and nonfigurative words, phrases, and statements in uncomplicated passages
24–27	Use context to determine the appropriate meaning of virtually any word, phrase, or statement in uncomplicated passages
	Use context to determine the appropriate meaning of some figurative and nonfigurative words, phrases, and statements in more challenging passages
28–32	Determine the appropriate meaning of words, phrases, or statements from figurative or somewhat technical contexts

In this chapter, you will review how to apply reading skills to determine the meanings of words, phrases, and statements. You will use your growing knowledge to analyze both uncomplicated and more challenging passages that contain figurative and nonfigurative language, descriptive language, and so on.

UNDERSTANDING WORDS AND PHRASES

In order to understand what you read, it is important to comprehend the **implication of words and phrases**. Many words and phrases are familiar. You easily recognize them and understand what they mean because you use, read, or hear them regularly. Others might be unfamiliar or could be specific only to the passage you are reading. Still, you will need to determine what these new words and phrases mean or imply in order to fully understand the passage.

Familiar Word or Phrase: "Come on! Get a little pep in your step!"

The phrase "Get a little pep in your step" is familiar to most people. They recognize it as an idiom that implies the person being spoken to needs to be more energetic.

Interpreting Words and Phrases

Unfamiliar Word or Phrase: "No worries, Annie. Saturn's not going anywhere."

– from *Promise Me the Moon* by Joyce Annette Barnes

The phrase above is not a common one. It comes from a short story about a girl who wants to grow up to be an astronaut. "Saturn's not going anywhere" is the speaker's way of saying that the planet will be there, waiting for Annie, no matter how long it takes her to realize her dream of going into space. From the context of the story, a reader can see that the speaker is encouraging Annie not to give up, even when it appears her dream is out of reach.

DESCRIPTIVE LANGUAGE

Descriptive language refers to words and phrases that are meant to help the reader *see* or *feel* a scene in the passage. Descriptive words include adjectives that help describe a person, place, idea, mood, or thing with a vividness that brings the text to life. Descriptive words also include verbs and adverbs that precisely describe a scene or action. Look at the sentences below, and note the descriptive words and phrases.

> With his catlike reflexes, Donovan sprang into action.

The fact that Donovan's reflexes are described as being *catlike* helps paint a picture of someone who is keenly aware of his surroundings and quick to react. The verb *sprang* precisely describes the rapid motion of someone reacting to a situation quickly and decisively.

> Bartholomew's troublesome news overshadowed the entire occasion.

The term *troublesome* suggests that Bartholomew's news is sad, disheartening, or upsetting. The term *overshadowed* communicates that the news is big enough to affect the mood of an entire event.

Entire excerpts of a passage can rely heavily on some form of descriptive language. Here is an example of a passage that relies on imagery. Imagery is the attempt to create a mental image for the reader by evoking one or more of the five senses. Authors use imagery to flesh out the world they create and to draw a reader in by giving them a sensuous, fully-developed sense of place. In *Ask the Dust*, author John Fante describes a busy Los Angeles intersection:

> And so I was down on Fifth and Olive, where the big street cars chewed your ears with their noise, and the smell of gasoline made the palm trees seem sad, and the black pavement was still wet from the fog of the night before.

Not surprisingly, this novel is famous for capturing the "feel" of living in California during the 1930s. In only a few words, Fante creates images which stimulate the reader's senses of sight, sound, smell, and touch. Notice how these few descriptive words give you the sense that you are standing on that busy street corner with the author as he lays down the setting for his story. He has established a certain mood through the language he uses, and the actions that occur in this setting retain this intentional feeling of strange desolation.

Chapter 4

FIGURATIVE LANGUAGE

The passage you just read contains subtle yet powerful imagery. Imagery is only one type of **figurative language**. This is language that is meant to represent an idea or illustrate a point. It is not meant to be taken as being literally true. Figurative language employs imaginative and often powerful words to express ideas and make a passage come alive. Below is a table consisting of some examples of figurative language.

\multicolumn{2}{c	}{**Figurative Language**}
Device	**Definition and Examples**
Allegory	a work in which the characters, setting, or events represent ideas or beliefs that are more than they appear to be on the surface; in an allegory, everything symbolically stands for something
	Examples: George Orwell's *Animal Farm* is a story about animals and a farmer on the surface but is really a look at the corruption of Stalin-era Russia; William Golding's *Lord of the Flies* is about a group of boys marooned on an island but is really about human nature and tensions between individuality and the common good.
Allusion	a reference to a well-known place, literary or art work, famous person, or historical event; in today's world, these references are often related to pop culture
	Example: You tell your friends that your nephew reminds you of Bart Simpson; if they know this character from the popular cartoon *The Simpsons*, they would have a picture of a wisecracking and misbehaving boy!
Analogy	an extended explanation or description of something unfamiliar or difficult to explain by comparison with something familiar
	Example: "Life is like a box of chocolates; you never know what you're going to get." – Forrest Gump
Hyperbole	exaggeration to create an effect
	Example: 1) I would rather die than eat brussels sprouts. 2) If you hum that tune one more time, I'll explode.
Imagery	the use of words or phrases that evoke the sensations of sight, hearing, touch, smell, or taste
	Example: Edgar Allan Poe opens "The Fall of the House of Usher" with "During the whole of a dull, dark, and soundless day in the autumn of the year, when the clouds hung oppressively low in the heavens ..." Poe's word choices help the reader picture the day and the mood.

Interpreting Words and Phrases

Irony	a contrast between expectation and reality; there are three common types of irony
	
	• **Verbal irony** involves a contrast between what is said or written and what is meant.
	    Example: After a day of mischief, little Juan was tired. With a smile, his mother put him down for a nap, cooing sweetly, "Now, you can rest, *my little angel.*"
	• **Situational irony** occurs when what happens is very different from what is expected to happen.
	    Example: In Aesop's fable "The Tortoise and the Hare," a tortoise wins a race of speed against a hare.
	• **Dramatic irony** occurs when the audience or the reader knows something a character does not know.
	    Example: In reading a tragic novel in which a character is ill and going to die, the reader might learn of the character's illness *before* the character does.

Metaphor	a direct comparison between two unlike things without using the words *like* or *as* **Examples:** 1) The sun was a ball of fire. 2) Life is but a dream.
Onomatopoeia	words that imitate the sound they are naming **Examples:** woof, meow, splash, boom, hiss, buzz, pitter-patter
Personification	giving human qualities to something not human **Examples:** 1) "Sky lowered, and muttering thunder, some sad drops / Wept at completing of the mortal sin." – John Milton, 2) "The oak trees whispered softly in the night breeze." – John Steinbeck
Simile	comparison between two things using *like* or *as* **Examples:** 1) "Sometimes I feel like a motherless child" –African American spiritual, 2) "My love is like a red, red rose" – Robert Burns
Symbolism	when any object, person, place, or action that has a meaning in itself and is also used to represent a meaning beyond itself, such as a quality, an attitude, a belief, or a value **Examples:** 1) A skull and crossbones are often a symbol that warns of poison. 2) A dove with an olive branch is a symbol of peace. 3) In Nathaniel Hawthorne's short story "The Minister's Black Veil," the black veil symbolizes secret sin.

Chapter 4

Read the passage below. Then review the analysis that follows about the figurative language in the passage.

> "I'm at my wit's end!" bellowed Bradley. "It would be easier to swim across a sea of man-eating sharks than to make Christina happy sometimes."
>
> "A woman is like a classical violin," sighed Uncle Charlie. "Beautiful, and full of sweet music if encouraged by one who knows how to help her play the right chords."

The first paragraph consists of a familiar phrase. ("I'm at my wit's end"). It communicates that Bradley is extremely frustrated and doesn't know what else to do. The paragraph also contains the use of hyperbole ("It would be easier to swim across a sea of man-eating sharks than to make Christina happy"). The statement is not meant to be taken as literally true. The character is frustrated in his relationship with a moody woman named Christina, and he is making an exaggerated statement to communicate how hard it is for him to please her.

The second paragraph makes use of an analogy. ("A woman is like a classical violin.") The simile compares a woman and a classical violin and is meant to communicate a point about how a man should interact with a woman. The phrase "Beautiful, and full of sweet music if encouraged by one who knows how to help her play the right chords" implies that Uncle Charlie is saying that a man has to know the right things to do in order to make Christina happy.

Interpreting Words and Phrases

Practice 1: Understanding Words and Phrases

Read the passage below. Then answer the questions that follow.

Excerpt from "Typhoon"
by Theodore Dreiser

There was no escape from the severe regimen Ida was compelled to follow. She had work to do; she had rules to observe. First, there was breakfast at seven-thirty sharp because the store had to be opened by her father at eight, which meant rising at seven; next, luncheon at twelve-thirty, so as to satisfy her father and her own noon recess hour which
5 was completely filled in by this; finally, dinner always at six-thirty because there were many things, commercial and social, which fell upon the shoulders of William Zobel at night. And between whiles, from four to six on weekdays and later from seven to ten at night, as well as all day Saturdays, there was store duty in her father's store.

While other girls walked the streets arm in arm, or made pairs with young men of the
10 region or elsewhere and were off to the movies, or to some party—and came in at what hours after—(didn't she hear them laugh and chatter at school and on their way home, afterwards)—she, because of her father's and later her step-mother's attitude, was compelled to adhere to the regimen thought advisable for her. No parties that kept her out later than ten at night at anytime— and then only after due investigation. Those she really
15 liked were always picked to pieces by her step-mother and, of course, this somewhat influenced the opinion of her father.

1. In the sentence that reads "There was no escape from the severe regimen Ida was compelled to follow," the phrase *severe regimen* means which of the following?

    A. Fun activity

    B. Strict schedule

    C. Relaxed atmosphere

    D. Cruel leader

2. The phrase "there were many things, commercial and social, which fell upon the shoulders of William Zobel at night" implies which of the following?

    A. William Zobel has many responsibilities at night.

    B. William Zobel is afraid of the nighttime.

    C. William Zobel has strong shoulders.

    D. William Zobel is the victim of a nighttime accident.

3. The language used in the second paragraph of the passage paints an image of Ida as someone who:

   A. is very happy with her life.

   B. wishes she were closer to her parents.

   C. envies the freedom and fun of others.

   D. is working hard to pursue a dream.

4. In the sentence that includes the phrase "Those she really liked were always picked to pieces by her step-mother," the phrase *picked to pieces* means which of the following?

   A. Ida's stepmother does not want her to see any boys.

   B. Ida's stepmother will not stop asking her questions about boys.

   C. Ida's stepmother enjoys flirting with boys Ida liked.

   D. Ida's stepmother is critical of boys Ida liked.

Read the passage below, and then answer the questions that follow.

Mowing the Grass—A Tragedy

One sunny day, Allen went outside to mow the lawn for his parents. This would be the first lawn of the day for him; he had a list of neighbors' yards to cut when he was finished with his own. His lawn service business was really taking off! Thinking about all he had to do, he quickly started the motor and began mowing. "I bet I can finish this whole lawn
5 in under thirty minutes!" Allen thought. But because he was mowing so quickly, Allen had not taken time to clear the yard of sticks and rocks before he started mowing. So he did not notice the large rock in the middle of the overgrown lawn. The rock entered his lawn mower with a "*bang, ka-chink!*" and broke apart the whirring blades. Sharp-edged rock fragments flung out from beneath the mower pelted Allen's ankles. He cried out, "Ouch!"
10 and stopped the growling lawn mower. He bent down to inspect the damage. His lower legs were speckled with red spots and scratches, and a stinging cut on his right ankle was bleeding freely. Then he saw the jagged rip across the side of his left track shoe. "Oh no, not my new shoes!" he exclaimed. "Man, I am all messed up." Then he turned over the mower and saw the mangled remains of the blade assembly, and his spirits sagged even
15 lower. "Now I won't be able to work for my paying customers today." Still, Allen tried to make light of the accident. "Wonder if my parents will pay me disability for this?" he said aloud and laughed regretfully. Then he limped inside to bandage himself up.

Interpreting Words and Phrases

5. In the story, the phrase "*bang, ka-chink!*" is used by the author to:

    A. describe how Allen feels when his lawnmower breaks.

    B. help the reader picture how badly Allen's ankle has been hurt.

    C. enable the reader to hear the sound of the lawnmower hitting the rock.

    D. help the reader understand Allen's disappointment at this situation.

6. Which of the following phrases best helps readers understand how Allen gets hurt?

    A. He cried out, "Ouch!" and stopped the growling lawn mower.

    B. "Wonder if my parents will pay me disability for this?" he said aloud and laughed regretfully.

    C. But because he was mowing so quickly, Allen had not taken time to clear the yard of sticks and rocks before he started mowing.

    D. Sharp-edged rock fragments flung out from beneath the mower pelted Allen's ankles.

UNDERSTANDING CONTEXT

One of the most effective means for determining the meaning of words and phrases in a passage is to look at the *context* in which it is used. The **context** of a word of phrase refers to the manner in which the author uses it and the role it plays in relation to the broader text.

In order to be prepared to do well on the PLAN Reading Test, you will need to be ready to **use context to determine the meaning of figurative and nonfigurative words, phrases, and statements in both uncomplicated and more challenging passages**.

Read the sentences below. See if you can determine the meaning of the italicized words based on the context in which the author uses them.

1. Green algae remain *dormant* until rains revive them.

    A. Dry

    B. Dead

    C. Small

    D. Inactive

2. *Aerobic* exercise increases your heart and breathing rates for a sustained period of time.

   A. Longlasting

   B. Strength training

   C. Requiring oxygen

   D. Demanding

If the italicized words in the examples are unfamiliar to you, you can determine their meanings in several ways. Using context clues is the most common strategy. In the first example, the clause "until rains revive them" suggests that *dormant* is not a dead state but an inactive one, since the rains make the algae active again. In addition, the signal word "until" tells us that *dormant* is the opposite of *revive*. When two words are compared in this way, it is called a **contrast clue**.

The second example indicates the definition of *aerobic* is described in the second part of the sentence. Since heart and breathing rates are increased, and all organisms need to breathe oxygen to live, *aerobic* must mean "requiring oxygen."

Below is a list of the main types of context clues alongside their signal words.

Context Clues	Signal Words
Comparison	*also, like, resembling, too, both, than* Look for clues that show how an unfamiliar word is similar to a familiar word or phrase. **Example:** The accident *felled* the utility pole like a tree for timber.
Contrast	*but, however, while, instead of, yet, unlike* Look for clues that indicate how an unfamiliar word is the opposite of a familiar word or phrase. **Example:** Stephanie is usually in a state of *composure*, but her sister is mostly boisterous.
Definition or Restatement	*is, or, that is, in other words, which* Look for words that define the term or restate it in other words. **Example:** The principal's idea is to *circuit*—or move around—the campus weekly to make sure everything is okay.
Example	*for example, for instance, such as* Look for examples used in context that reveal the meaning of an unfamiliar word. **Example:** People use all sorts of *vehicles* such as cars, bicycles, rickshaws, airplanes, boats, and motorcycles.

Interpreting Words and Phrases

Some questions on the PLAN Reading Test could require you to **determine appropriate meaning of words, phrases, or statements from figurative or somewhat technical context.**

Below is an example passage. Read the text, and note the comments that follow regarding its meaning based on context.

> My fate was set. My path marked out for me—a path I did not choose or want. Ah, to be one of those blackbirds overhead. Away they went. To where, I don't know. I only know they came and went as they chose, flying high and far from here when the impulse hit them.

Based on the context, what is the purpose of the phrase "Ah, to be one of those blackbirds"? A close reading of the entire text reveals that the phrase uses figurative language to express the narrator's desire to be free from whatever fate and path he is referring to.

Practice 2: Understanding Context

For each sentence, choose the answer whose meaning is closest to the italicized word. Use context clues to help you.

1. The smell of fried fish *permeated* the whole house.

    A. Jammed

    B. Shook

    C. Filled

    D. Colored

2. Hank said the ocean was very *tranquil*; I also thought the ocean was peaceful.

    A. Calm

    B. Pretty

    C. Clear

    D. Shiny

3. Eating too much candy is likely to have a *pernicious* effect on one's health; they don't call it "junk food" for nothing.

    A. Large

    B. Lasting

    C. Negative

    D. Creative

Chapter 4

4. As the snow *accumulates*, traveling the roads becomes more dangerous.

   A. Dissolves

   B. Increases

   C. Moves

   D. Transfers

5. To drive home his point, John once again *reiterated* the facts regarding the trial.

   A. Investigated

   B. Planned

   C. Rehearsed

   D. Repeated

Read the passage below, and then answer the questions that follow.

Stone by Stone: The Great Wall of China

In the distant reach of time in the Far East, China's culture was already highly developed and thriving. With success and plenty, there often comes division between people. Some groups of people struggle to hold on to what they have created, while other people struggle to be a part of the success. This is how, in the seventh century BC, the Great
5 Wall began.

The wall actually began as simple earthworks, piles of dirt and rock placed in areas which were open to invasion. The first known part of the wall created as a permanent structure was built in the state of Ch'u. Other states saw the building of the wall, and they saw that it was good. The wall served as an early warning station for lookouts standing
10 high on platforms. The wall was also easy to defend: arrows and other weapons could be fired from above—down upon any invading forces.

Little can be known about the personal lives of the earliest builders of the wall. It is believed that the wall was built under the direction of both military force as well as a cultural force. These influences directed the people to obey for the greater good of the
15 community.

Each of the walls, built by different states, finally were connected during the Qin dynasty (221–207 BC). A dynasty is a family of rulers who inherit power through its bloodline, thereby ruling over a country for generations. The construction of the wall improved. The materials used in the process of connecting the walls were not mere piles
20 of earth and stones, but brick and granite. During the Ming dynasty (AD 1368–1644), the

Interpreting Words and Phrases

wall was carefully built up with watchtowers and structural designs that benefited the military and pleased the eye. These elements of beauty and defense symbolized the grandeur of the Chinese empire.

6. According to the passage, the wall was built largely for what reason?

    A. To honor the emperor

    B. To provide defense

    C. To honor gods

    D. To make money

7. Which of the following statements suggests that the wall was a magnificent and strong construction?

    A. The wall actually began as simple earthworks, piles of dirt and rock placed in areas which were open to invasion.

    B. It is believed that the wall was built under the direction of both military force as well as a cultural force.

    C. Each of the walls, built by different states, finally were connected during the Qin dynasty.

    D. These elements of beauty and defense symbolized the grandeur of the Chinese empire.

Read the passage below, and then answer the questions that follow.

Philip ran his fingers over the old hat. He couldn't begin to recount all the times he'd seen his Pa Pa tug at its bill or pull it low over his eyes when they were fishing. A smile broke through the quiet tears that made their way down his cheeks as he thought about the times his Pa Pa had placed the hat on Philip's little head and laughed "There ya go, Partna."
5 Let the others squabble over his grandfather's little bit of money, old aluminum boat, and tiny, three-bedroom house. All he wanted was that hat—just that one old, dirt-stained John Deere hat.

8. In the passage above, the hat serves as:

    A. a symbol of the grandfather's memory.

    B. an object the family is squabbling over.

    C. Philip's grandfather's prized possession.

    D. something Philip had forgotten about.

9. In the passage, the term "Partna" serves as which of the following?

   A. An expression of disappointment

   B. A description of Philip

   C. A show of affection

   D. A nickname for the grandfather

Read the passage below, and then answer the questions that follow.

It is important that our meetings are conducted with structure and order. Therefore, there is a specific protocol for speaking during a meeting. If there is something you would like to share, then you must first secure your right to the floor. To do this, raise your hand, and then sit quietly. When she is ready, our moderator will call on you. Once the moderator
5 recognizes you, you may then stand and have the floor. When you are finished, please sit down again, and relinquish the floor to the moderator. The moderator will then open the floor for any comments or possible opposing views.

10. According to the passage, the phrase *securing the floor* means:

    A. you have something to say.

    B. you have been given the right to speak.

    C. you are upset about something.

    D. you want to take the place of the moderator.

11. According to the passage, the moderator is:

    A. someone with an opposing view.

    B. an elected officer in the group.

    C. someone in charge of the meeting.

    D. an individual who desperately wants the floor.

Interpreting Words and Phrases

CHAPTER 4 SUMMARY

Below are some key concepts covered in chapter 4 and some of the reading comprehension skills you need to be prepared to demonstrate on the PLAN Reading Test.

Understand the implications of words and phrases.

Understand the implications of simple descriptive language.

Use context to understand basic figurative language.

Use context to determine the appropriate meaning of some figurative and nonfigurative words, phrases, and statements.

Determine the appropriate meaning of words, phrases, or statements from figurative or somewhat technical contexts.

CHAPTER 4 REVIEW

Below is a passage. The questions that follow will allow you to practice the skills covered in this chapter and listed at the beginning of this chapter review.

PROSE FICTION: The following is excerpted from "The Red-Headed League," one of the numerous Sherlock Holmes stories by Sir Arthur Conan Doyle. Dr. John Watson, friend of Sherlock Holmes, is the narrator of this story. Watson has arrived at Holmes's apartment while Holmes is meeting with a client.

The portly client puffed out his chest with an appearance of some little pride and pulled a dirty and wrinkled newspaper from the inside pocket of his
5   coat. As he glanced down the advertisement column..., I took a good look at the man and endeavored, after the fashion of my companion, to read the indications which might be presented by
10 his dress or appearance.

I did not gain very much, however, by my inspection. Our visitor bore every mark of being an average British tradesman, obese, pompous, and slow.
15 He wore rather baggy gray trousers, a not very clean black coat, unbuttoned in the front, and a drab waistcoat with a heavy brassy chain and a square bit of metal dangling down as an ornament. A frayed
20 top-hat and a faded brown overcoat with a wrinkled velvet collar lay upon a chair beside him. Altogether, look as I would, there was nothing remarkable about the man save his blazing red head, and the
25 expression of extreme chagrin and discontent upon his features.

Sherlock Holmes's quick eye took in my occupation, and he shook his head with a smile as he noticed my
30 questioning glances. "Beyond the obvious facts that he has at some time done manual labor, that he takes snuff, that he is a Freemason, that he has been in China and that he has done a
35 considerable amount of writing lately, I can deduce nothing else."

Chapter 4

Mr. Jabez Wilson started up in his chair, with his forefinger upon the paper, but his eyes upon my companion.

40 "How, in the name of good-fortune, did you know all that, Mr. Holmes?" he asked. "How did you know, for example, that I did manual labor. It's as true as gospel, for I began as a ship's carpenter."

45 "Your hands, my dear sir. Your right hand is quite a size larger than your left. You have worked with it, and the muscles are more developed."

"Well, the snuff, then, and the
50 Freemasonry?"

"I won't insult your intelligence by telling you how I read that, especially as, rather against the strict rules of your order, you use an arc-and-compass
55 breastpin."

"Ah, of course, I forgot that. But the writing?"

"What else can be indicated by that right cuff so very shiny for five inches,
60 and the left one with the smooth patch near the elbow where you rest it upon the desk?"

"Well, but China?"

"The fish that you have tattooed
65 immediately above your right wrist could only have been done in China. I have made a small study of tattoo marks and have even contributed to the literature of the subject. That trick of
70 staining the fishes' scales a delicate pink is quite peculiar to China. When, in addition, I see a Chinese coin hanging from your watch-chain, the matter becomes even more simple."

75 Mr. Jabez Wilson laughed heavily. "Well, I never!" said he. "I thought at first that you had done something clever, but I see that there was nothing in it, after all."

80 "I begin to think, Watson," said Holmes, "that I make a mistake in explaining… My poor little reputation, such as it is, will suffer shipwreck if I am so candid."

1. What does the word *peculiar* mean in line 71?

    A. Ordinary

    B. Particular to that area

    C. Cloudy and uncertain

    D. Malformed or disfigured

2. As it is used in line 36, what does the word *deduce* mean?

    F. Believe

    G. Figure out

    H. Put up with

    J. Common sense

3. Holmes's phrase in lines 82–84, "My poor little reputation…will suffer shipwreck if I am so candid," means that:

    A. he is worried that his reputation will suffer if his predictions about his clients are wrong.

    B. he thinks that Watson and Mr. Wilson don't understand his explanations.

    C. he thinks that Watson is better at observing people than he is.

    D. he is worried that his reputation will suffer if he gives away his secrets too freely.

Interpreting Words and Phrases

4. Based on the description of the man in the second paragraph, what does Watson most likely think of Wilson?

   F. He thinks he is very clean and tidy in his appearance.

   G. He thinks he is a shady criminal.

   H. He thinks he is very intelligent and clever.

   J. He thinks he looks like the typical British working-class person.

5. Doyle writes in line 38 that Mr. Wilson "started up in his chair" when Holmes reveals the facts he has deduced. Wilson's reaction indicates that initially Holmes's assessment of him has:

   A. offended him.

   B. bored him.

   C. amazed him.

   D. confused him.

6. Watson's statement in the opening paragraph that he "endeavored, after the fashion of my companion, to read the indications which might be presented by his dress or appearance" indicates that Watson is:

   F. suspicious of Wilson.

   G. attempting to imitate Sherlock Holmes.

   H. waiting for Holmes to express an opinion.

   J. unimpressed with Wilson.

Chapter 5
Generalizations and Conclusions

Some questions on the PLAN Reading Test will require you to draw **generalizations and conclusions** about people and ideas. You also may need to draw generalizations and conclusions using details that support the main point of more challenging passages. In this chapter, you will review how to draw generalizations and conclusions from information available in written passages.

These questions on the PLAN Reading Test will earn points based on the following scale, ranging from understanding implications of familiar language to determining meanings in more challenging passages.

13–15	Draw simple generalizations and conclusions about the main characters in uncomplicated literary narratives
16–19	Draw simple generalizations and conclusions about people, ideas, and so on in uncomplicated passages
20–23	Draw generalizations and conclusions about people, ideas, and so on in uncomplicated passages
	Draw simple generalizations and conclusions using details that support the main points of more challenging passages
24–27	Draw subtle generalizations and conclusions about characters, ideas, and so on in uncomplicated literary narratives
	Draw generalizations and conclusions about people, ideas, and so on in more challenging passages
28–32	Use information from one or more sections of a more challenging passage to draw generalizations and conclusions about people, ideas, and so on

DRAWING GENERALIZATIONS

A **generalization** is an inference that a reader draws from a passage. It involves evaluating facts and details and then applying these points to broader situations that are sometimes similar. Read the sentence below, and then review the analysis that follows.

> The girls in that club can be extremely cruel; they often engage in hurtful gossip.

Based on the sentence above, you get the impression that all the girls who belong to the club to which the author refers are likely to engage in hurtful gossip. The statement has led you to make a generalization about all girls in the club. In reality, some of the girls in the club might not behave this way. The statement is a generalization.

Generalizations and Conclusions

You could encounter a question on the PLAN requiring you to **draw a simple generalization about the main character**. Read the passage below, and then answer the question that follows.

> Robert had a love-hate relationship with spring. He loved the warmer weather and taking walks through the woods observing the beauty of the outdoors. But he could barely survive the pollen. Without his allergy medicine, he dared not hike so much as around the block. He never ventured outside the house at this time of year without having taken his
> 5 medication. This is how it had been for years. He was certainly used to it.

According to the passage, it is likely that Robert will do which of the following before going on a hike?

A. He will pack a backpack.

B. He will walk the length of a football field.

C. He will take his allergy medicine.

D. He will see a doctor about his allergies.

Answer C is correct. The passage clearly states that Robert never ventures outside in the springtime without taking his allergy medicine. Therefore, the reader can draw the generalization that Robert would most likely take his allergy medicine before going on a hike. True, Robert might pack a backpack. But the passage says nothing about a backpack, and so the reader cannot draw this generalization. (Answer A is eliminated.) The passage says that Robert dares not hike around the block without taking his medicine. It does not say that he would likely walk the length of a football field before going on a hike. (Answer B is eliminated.) Although Robert might go see a doctor, nothing in the passage suggests that he has any plans to. Therefore, the reader cannot draw this generalization. (Answer D is eliminated.)

Some questions on the PLAN could require you to **draw a simple generalization about people, ideas, and so on**. Read the short passage below, and then answer the question that follows.

> Often, students must deal with stress in their daily lives. The sources of this stress may be academic, emotional, or physical. Many students develop positive ways to cope with this stress.

According to the passage, which of the following situations most likely would cause stress?

A. Taking a summer vacation

B. Studying for a final exam

C. Eating your favorite breakfast

D. Reading a comic book

Answer B is correct. Using the information available in the passage, the reader can draw the generalization that exams are likely to cause stress. Why? The passage states that many students deal with stress and that one source of stress is academic pressure. The other two possible causes mentioned in the passage are emotional and physical stresses. Since summer vacations, eating your favorite breakfast, and reading a comic book all tend to be relaxing and enjoyable activities that do not qualify as academic, emotional, or physical stress, we cannot draw a generalization that any of these activities would be a source of stress. (Answers A, C, and D are eliminated.)

Some questions might require you to **draw simple generalizations using details that support the main point of a passage**. Read the passage below, and then answer the question that follows.

Native Americans Prior to European Colonization

Centuries before Europeans reached North America, the first inhabitants of the continent migrated from Asia, probably across a "land bridge" between Siberia and Alaska that was exposed during the earth's last Ice Age. These people, referred to as Native Americans, established the first societies in North America. Some even established
5   sophisticated civilizations that were advanced in art, science, technology, and agriculture. For instance, the Mayas (AD 300–900) of present-day Yucatan and Guatemala were so advanced in science and mathematics that they were among the first to introduce the concept of "zero" and actually developed a calendar more accurate than those in Europe. Later, the Aztecs (1325–1519) of central Mexico ruled an empire of between 5 and 20
10   million people prior to being conquered by the Spanish. Because they were able to adopt and expand on much of the art, religion, and technology they inherited from earlier civilizations, the Aztecs are often compared to the ancient Romans who inherited and expanded upon the accomplishments of the early Greeks.

According to the passage, which of the following is true?

A. Early American inhabitants had sophisticated civilizations.

B. Europeans had more advanced culture than Native Americans.

C. Early Native Americans were descendants of ancient Romans.

D. Mayas and Aztecs were related to tribes from Alaska or Siberia.

Answer A is correct. The passage states that some early Native American cultures established sophisticated civilizations. It goes on to support this by describing how the Mayan and Aztec cultures embraced science, mathematics, art, religion, and technology. The reader can draw the generalization that these cultures were sophisticated people. The passage does not compare the early Europeans to the Native American cultures, so the reader cannot draw the generalization that their culture was more advanced. (Answer B is eliminated.) The passage does not claim that Native Americans are descendants of the Romans, but suggests that they are often compared to the Romans. (Answer C is eliminated.) The passage says that early Native Americans probably crossed a land bridge between Siberia and Alaska, but this was long before the Mayas or Aztecs. The reader cannot assume that the Mayas or Aztecs came from Alaska or Siberia. (Answer D is eliminated.)

Generalizations and Conclusions

Other questions might require you to **draw subtle generalizations about characters and ideas, based on details in an uncomplicated literary narrative**. Read the passage below, and then answer the question that follows.

    Melinda held tightly to the back of the truck, her helmet and fireproof coat almost engulfing her tiny frame. "Now we'll find out what the little girl is made of," she heard Bruce snicker, eliciting a laugh from Jensen. Burying the comment, Melinda focused. This was her first real fire. This was her first chance to prove herself. All the doubting looks and
5 all the mean, sexist comments would be vanquished if she could just hold her own and prove her merit on this call.

According to the passage, which of the following statements best describes the way in which the male firefighters regard Melinda?

A. They respect her for her bravery in the face of danger.

B. They feel protective toward her because she's a girl.

C. They worry that she is a better firefighter than they are.

D. They look down on her because she's a woman.

Answer D is correct. Bruce's sarcastic statement, Jensen's snickering, and the facts that Melinda has endured doubting looks and sexist comments and feels the need to prove herself are all details that allow the reader to draw the generalization that the male firefighters Melinda works with look down on her because she's a woman. There is nothing in the passage to suggest the male firefighters respect her or are protective of her. (Answers A and B are eliminated.) The fact that Bruce says, "Now we'll find out what the little girl's made of" also suggests that he questions her abilities rather than fearing that she might be a better firefighter than he. (Answer C is eliminated.)

Still other passages might require you to **use information from one or more sections of a more challenging passage to draw generalizations**. Read the passage below, and then answer the question that follows.

Chronicles of a Crazy Day

    It all started when I helped someone in trouble. Believe me. There was so much crowding and hurrying in the hall that someone was bound to trip. That person was Anya, my friend from Peer Helpers Club. Well, what was I supposed to do? I dropped all my things and helped her up. Then we had to collect the myriad and somewhat peculiar
5 contents of her notebook, which had spilled out as a result of her fall. Anya is not terribly organized, but she's really smart—and interesting. She really is.

    "Thanks," she said, smiling ruefully as I helped her rescue the scattered collection of sushi-shaped erasers now threatening to migrate to parts unknown under a parade of shuffling and stumbling feet headed for classes.

Chapter 5

10   "No problem," I laughed. "But I have to rush. Science class." I grabbed my stuff off the floor and headed for Hall B.

Halfway through science, I realized my shoe bag was missing! It had my soccer cleats in it. I must have left it on the hall floor!

The bell rang. I had to find my cleats before catching the bus home. I had a test to
15 study for and a game to play. I rushed to the office. No one had seen a shoe bag with cleats in it. I had to go from room to room looking for them. I finally found them, but not until after the buses had left!

I called home. My parents were at work, so there was no one to pick me up. I had to walk the two miles home, but I made it. My feet were sore. My shins ached. I was not
20 inspired by the thought of playing soccer. But it was already time to go to the game.

I got a ride to the field, but my legs were so tired, I tended to trip a lot. Once, I fell on the ball just as another player was trying to kick it. Instead, his cleated foot found my lower right arm.

I tried to tell Coach that it wasn't serious. But my inability to breathe made my act
25 unconvincing. Before I knew it, I was at the hospital.

Four hours later, I returned home, arm in a cast and unable to write—even if I could think straight on all those painkillers. That is why, Ms. Sweeney, I was not able to study for today's social studies test. I hope you will grant me a two-day grace period before I am required to take it. And I promise to stay away from crowded hallways!

According to the passage, crowded school hallways:

A. are good places to meet new people.

B. are places where accidents are likely to happen.

C. are the busiest places in any modern school.

D. are likely to interfere with athletic events.

Answer B is correct. Details throughout the passage allow the reader to draw the generalization that hallways are likely places for accidents. They include the narrator's statement that "someone was bound to trip," the fact that Anya did trip, and the narrator's promise to "stay away from crowded hallways." The passage does not describe the narrator meeting anyone new in the hallway; he already knew Anya. (Answer A is eliminated.) Although incidents in the crowded hallway certainly could lead to someone getting hurt, one cannot draw the generalization that hallways are the busiest places in all schools. (Answer C is eliminated.) Although the day's events did interfere with the narrator's normal participation in his soccer game, the reader cannot draw the generalization that crowded hallways alone are likely to interfere with athletic events. (Answer D is eliminated.)

Generalizations and Conclusions

Practice 1: Drawing Generalizations

Read the passages below, and then answer the questions that follow.

The Hermit's Hut

Thomas, bearing the unconscious monk in his arms and somewhat faint from his own wounds, staggered in the direction of the chiming bell. He had but a short distance to go from the scene of combat to the tiny chapel where a hermit was saying his prayers. At the sound of Thomas' clattering footsteps, the hermit turned with a start and hastened toward
5   him disclosing a kindly face lit by large brown eyes.

"Brother," gasped Thomas, "here is a holy man badly wounded for my sake. I beg you to use your skill with herbs to heal him."

The hermit responded quickly and led them into his chambers. Thomas carried the monk with tenderness and laid him down on the hermit's couch.

10   "I best be alone with him," said the hermit. "Go outside and wait till I come to you. I think the brother is not wounded unto death."

Thomas went out obediently as the good monk faintly called his name. "Be not troubled," said the hermit. "He does not know that he calls you. He is delirious." Alone with the monk, the hermit began to look at the wound. The hermit looked at the soft white
15   flesh of the shoulder with surprise. Then on impulse, he removed the hood and confirmed his thought. Long hair cascaded over the monk's delicate face. The hermit paused, looking at her frail body in dismay.

1. Based on the passage, which of the following generalizations is true?

   A. All hermits can heal sick people with herbs.

   B. When people help you, you should try to help them also.

   C. All monks are trained to fight in battles.

   D. When you are seriously injured, you can also be delirious.

Enough Adventure for One Day

"The next time you have any great ideas for raft engineering, keep them for the science fair," grumbled Anastasia LaPort, as she dipped the bucket lid into the murky river water, trying hopelessly to paddle. Beau, her twelve-year-old brother, who came up with new schemes every week, fancied himself as Huck Finn today. But his raft pole had broken ten
5   minutes ago, and the swampy river seemed to have devised its own ideas about their destination.

Normally ready with a clever argument for his sister, Beau remained silent. A kind of pressure clutched at his chest and throat. He wasn't sure whether it was the shifting boards beneath his bare feet, or the slithering movement he had just noticed along the bank about
10   fifty feet ahead that had caught his breath. But for once, he was speechless.

86

"Wait." He heard his sister's voice breaking the tension. "There's a tree trunk ahead. Let's try to grab onto it and walk it to shore." Beau looked up. She was right. Their one hope of escape lay ahead.

About forty feet ahead.

2. Which of the following is a generalization the author uses in the passage above?

   A. Boys are not good raft captains.

   B. Sisters are constantly mad at their brothers.

   C. Alligators often lie in wait along banks of rivers.

   D. You should always raft where there are tree trunks.

DRAWING CONCLUSIONS

A conclusion is another type of inference. You **draw conclusions** when you use details in a passage to form a judgment or opinion about something not directly stated. Read the sentence below, and then review the analysis that follows.

> Hearing his name called from the stage, Jeffrey stood in his cap and gown, ready to claim that dream which he had spent four years of college working toward.

Based on the details in this sentence, the reader can conclude that Jeffrey is proud and relieved to be getting his college degree. The sentence does not directly state this fact; but the details in the sentence give readers enough information to draw this conclusion.

Some questions on the PLAN Reading Test will require you to **draw simple conclusions about the main characters in uncomplicated literary narratives**. For example, read the passage below, and answer the question that follows.

> Maria has studied all week for her algebra test. She spent three hours every night working on the review exercises in her textbook. Last night she could not sleep very well because she was afraid she would sleep through her alarm.

Which is a valid conclusion?

A. Maria will pass her test.

B. Maria is nervous about her algebra test.

C. Maria gets nervous before big tests.

D. Maria enjoys taking tests.

Generalizations and Conclusions

Maria is the main character in the passage. Based on Maria's actions (the amount of time she spends working on the review exercises and the fact that she cannot sleep for fear of sleeping through her alarm), the reader can conclude that Maria is nervous about her algebra test. The passage does not specifically say that she is nervous, but it does provide information that allows the reader to conclude this fact.

Some questions on the PLAN will require you to **draw conclusions about people, ideas, and so on in uncomplicated passages and more challenging passages**. Read the passage below, and then answer the questions that follow.

The Theory of Birth Order

According to some psychologists, the order in which you were born can help determine your personality. Where you are in the family plays a large role in determining the relationship between you and your parents and between you and your siblings. Those family relationships can also set the pattern for the way you will respond to people later in
5 life. Psychologists have come to certain conclusions about behavior according to your birth order.

Oldest children tend to be responsible, productive, independent, and obedient. They are bolder and often take on leadership roles. Oldest children are typically well organized, precise, and prone to perfectionism. Middle children are negotiators. They can be very
10 easygoing. Middle children often make a place for themselves outside the family. Because they tend to go out on their own, middle children are often the most creative. Youngest children are usually affectionate, sensitive, dependent, and charming. They are used to being taken care of and often become attention seeking or manipulative.

Of course, personality development is not explained completely by birth order, but
15 studying the effects of birth order can give you insight into how the forces within families shape children.

According to the passage, if you visited a conference of civic leaders, you might conclude that the audience there would be mostly made up of people who had been:

A. the youngest children in their families.

B. the middle children in their families.

C. the oldest children in their families.

D. only children who had no siblings.

Answer C is correct. The passage states that older children are the ones more prone to take on leadership roles. Therefore you could conclude that out of a room full of civic leaders, most would be oldest children. Middle and youngest children are not found to normally exhibit strong leadership traits. (Answers A and B are eliminated.) The passage makes no reference to only children. (Answer D is eliminated.)

Chapter 5

Which conclusion would you make about the career a middle child is most likely to choose?

A. Nurse

B. Artist

C. Accountant

D. Mathematician

Answer B is correct. The passage says that middle children are often the most creative. Since being an artist is the most creative occupation listed, you could conclude that the middle child would most likely choose that profession. Since youngest children tend to be the most affectionate and sensitive, you could conclude that they would most likely choose being a nurse. (Answer A is eliminated.) Since the passage suggest that oldest children are more likely to be precise and value perfectionism, you could conclude that they would be more likely to be an accountant or a mathematician. (Answers C and D are eliminated.)

Other questions on the PLAN will require you to **draw simple conclusions using details that support the main points of more challenging passages**. Read the passage below, and then answer the question that follows.

Excerpt from *The Declaration of Independence*

We hold these truths to be self-evident, that all men are created equal, that they are endowed by their Creator with certain unalienable Rights, that among these are Life, Liberty and the pursuit of Happiness…. And for the support of this
5 Declaration, with a firm reliance on the protection of Divine Providence, we mutually pledge to each other our Lives, our Fortunes, and our sacred Honor.

Which of the following is a valid conclusion that can be drawn from the passage?

A. No one should be oppressed or kept from seeking a fulfilling life.

B. People must help one another to find contentment and success.

C. Religion helps people to be kind and helpful to each other.

D. Fighting for what you believe in is easier if you have an army.

Answer A is correct. This part of the document points out rights and freedoms of the country's citizens and that they should live free from domination by their government. While the concept of people helping each other is a fine ideal, this is not referred to in the passage. (Answer B is eliminated.) There is a short mention of "Divine Providence," but this passage is not about religion. (Answer C is eliminated.) The passage states that the signers pledge their lives, fortunes and honor, but there is no explicit mention of fighting for freedom. It is simply stated that these basic human rights exist and should be respected. (Answer D is eliminated.)

Generalizations and Conclusions

You could encounter questions on the PLAN that require you to **draw subtle generalizations and conclusions about characters, ideas, and so on in uncomplicated literary narratives.** You could also be required to **use information from one or more sections of a more challenging passage to draw conclusions about people, ideas, and so on**. Read the passages below, and then answer the questions that follow.

The First Woman

Once there was a beautiful woman who lived in a pleasant valley on the earth. She was the first of her kind to walk the face of the earth, and her life was sweet. The rest of the world was filled with forests, meadows, and mountains. In this valley, summer was the ruling season, and honey and fruit were always available. Her only companions were the
5 dove and the doe. She was the reigning spirit of this world, and nothing ever grew old or died.

One morning, the woman followed a scarlet butterfly to a remote waterfall, where the butterfly disappeared. Realizing she was lost, the woman fell asleep from exhaustion. When she woke, a being like herself stooped down and lifted her off the ground. Clothed
10 in a robe of clouds, the man-being told her he had seen her as he traveled across the sky.

Because he rescued her, the man-being had broken the commandment of the Great Spirit. For that, the man-being would remain on earth and share her companionship. For many moons, they lived happily in the valley. The woman bore a child. Sad because he had broken the law of the all-high, the man sought the guidance and forgiveness of the Great
15 Spirit. The Great Spirit took pity on the man and the woman. He opened up many more valleys and plains for the future inhabitants of the earth, but because of the broken commandment, the Great Spirit caused the man and woman to labor for their food. They would also suffer from cold, grow old, and die when their heads became as white as the feathers of swans.

What conclusion can you draw from the passage?

A. It is a true story.

B. The woman is a princess.

C. It is an ancient Tibetan story.

D. It is a myth to explain nature.

Answer D is correct. The passage tells a story that explains the cycle of life from the origins of the seasons to the reasons why people must work, grow old, and die. Therefore, you can conclude that it is a myth meant to explain nature. Although in the past some people may have accepted this story as being factual, most people today would see it as fiction. (Answer A is eliminated.) The passage suggests that the woman in the story is the first woman to ever live. Therefore, since she had no parents before her, she could not be a princess because that would make her the daughter of a king or queen. (Answer B is eliminated.) While the passage is an old story containing elements common to many early cultures, it cannot be stated for certain

90

Chapter 5

which culture is the source. The term "Great Spirit" is a ceremonial title used in Native American culture, but there is not enough evidence given in the passage to conclude that this story is Native American in origin, let alone Tibetan. (Answer C is eliminated.)

The Tao of Rice

by S. A. Snyder

Scott swerved his Honda 350 on the jungle path, narrowly missing a green mamba, one of the most poisonous snakes in Africa. I clutched his waist tighter. The dense, green tangle on both sides of us blurred as we passed, like a cartoon tunnel carrying us from the real world into a dream. Beige cement buildings appeared out of nowhere among the trees
5 and vines, as if we had discovered some lost civilization. This was the sprawling village of Diourou in southern Senegal, near where I would be living for the next two years.

We pulled up to Jean's house where a dozen children and adults milled about. Scott had taught Jean how to plant mango seedlings and start his own orchard. He wanted to show me the orchard to give me a feel for the work ahead.

10 "*Kasumay*," they said as we approached. Peace.

"*Kasumay keb*," we replied. Peace only.

Scott introduced us. I panicked and fell back on sketchy French, hoping they could understand.

Jean walked us through a maze of corridors inside his dark, cool house to the kitchen.
15 His mother, Inay, appeared from a back doorway, clutching a chicken by its legs. It hung motionless, then flapped its wings and squawked when she carelessly tossed it aside. She smiled at us and squawked too.

"*Kasumay!*"

"*Kasumay keb*," we replied. Jean and Scott told Inay who I was and what my mission
20 in Senegal was. She smiled and laughed, but threw me suspicious glances. Then Jean quietly conferred with Inay, who listened intently before knitting her brows and screeching an angry reply. Scott looked at me. My eyes begged for translation. Several minutes of negotiation passed between Inay and Jean. Scott gave me a quick translation.

– reprinted from *The Great Adventure: Volunteer Stories of Life Overseas* by the Peace Corps

Based on the details in the passage, the reader can draw which of these conclusions?

A. Green mambas live throughout Africa.

B. The narrator is new to Diourou.

C. The narrator is unfamiliar with the term *Kasumay*.

D. Jean is not fond of Scott.

Generalizations and Conclusions

Answer B is correct. Several facts support the conclusion that the narrator is new to Diourou: Scott has to explain to the narrator the work she will be doing as he shows her the orchard for the first time; he has to introduce the narrator to his regular acquaintances; the narrator is met with suspicious glances; and the narrator has yet to master the language and so must fall back on her "sketchy French." The passage also states that green mambas are among the most poisonous snakes in Africa, but the reader cannot conclude from this one remark that this species lives throughout the continent of Africa. (Answer A is eliminated.) The passage does not indicate that the narrator is unfamiliar with the term *Kasumay*. (Answer C is eliminated.) The passage indicates that Scott and Jean know each other and that Jean welcomes Scott's visits, and it goes further to explain how Scott has taught Jean how to plant mango seedlings and start his own orchard. These facts suggest that Jean has a good relationship with Scott. (Answer D is eliminated.)

Practice 2: Drawing Conclusions

Read the passages below. The questions that follow will allow you to practice the skills covered in this chapter and listed at the beginning of this chapter review.

PROSE FICTION: This passage is excerpted from "The White Heron" by Sarah Orne Jewett (1886).

The companions followed the shady wood-road, the cow taking slow steps and the child very fast ones. The cow stopped long at the brook to drink, as if the pasture were not half a swamp, and Sylvia stood still and waited, letting her bare feet cool themselves in the shoal water, while the great twilight moths struck softly against her. She waded on through
5 the brook as the cow moved away, and listened to the thrushes with a heart that beat fast with pleasure. There was a stirring in the great boughs overhead. They were full of little birds and beasts that seemed to be wide awake, and going about their world, or else saying goodnight to each other in sleepy twitters. Sylvia herself felt sleepy as she walked along. However, it was not much farther to the house, and the air was soft and sweet. She was not
10 often in the woods so late as this, and it made her feel as if she were a part of the gray shadows and the moving leaves. She was just thinking how long it seemed since she first came to the farm a year ago, and wondering if everything went on in the noisy town just the same as when she was there, the thought of the great red-faced boy who used to chase and frighten her made her hurry along the path to escape from the shadow of the trees.

15 Suddenly this little woods-girl is horror-stricken to hear a clear whistle not very far away. Not a bird's-whistle, which would have a sort of friendliness, but a boy's whistle, determined, and somewhat aggressive. Sylvia left the cow to whatever sad fate might await her, and stepped discreetly aside into the bushes, but she was just too late. The enemy had discovered her, and called out in a very cheerful and persuasive tone, "Halloa, little
20 girl, how far is it to the road?" and trembling Sylvia answered almost inaudibly, "A good ways."

She did not dare to look boldly at the tall young man, who carried a gun over his shoulder, but she came out of her bush and again followed the cow, while he walked alongside.

Chapter 5

"I have been hunting for some birds," the stranger said kindly, "and I have lost my way, and need a friend very much. Don't be afraid," he added gallantly. "Speak up and tell me what your name is, and whether you think I can spend the night at your house, and go out gunning early in the morning."

Sylvia was more alarmed than before. Would not her grandmother consider her much to blame? But who could have foreseen such an accident as this? It did not seem to be her fault, and she hung her head as if the stem of it were broken, but managed to answer, "Sylvy," with much effort when her companion again asked her name.

Mrs. Tilley was standing in the doorway when the trio came into view. The cow gave a loud moo by way of explanation.

"Yes, you'd better speak up for yourself, you old trial! Where'd she tucked herself away this time, Sylvy?" But Sylvia kept an awed silence; she knew by instinct that her grandmother did not comprehend the gravity of the situation. She must be mistaking the stranger for one of the farmer-lads of the region.

The young man stood his gun beside the door, and dropped a lumpy game-bag beside it; then he bade Mrs. Tilley good-evening, and repeated his wayfarer's story, and asked if he could have a night's lodging.

"Put me anywhere you like," he said. "I must be off early in the morning, before day; but I am very hungry, indeed. You can give me some milk at any rate, that's plain."

"Dear sakes, yes," responded the hostess, whose long slumbering hospitality seemed to be easily awakened. "You might fare better if you went out to the main road a mile or so, but you're welcome to what we've got. I'll milk right off, and you make yourself at home. You can sleep on husks or feathers," she proffered graciously. "I raised them all myself. There's good pasturing for geese just below here towards the ma'sh. Now step round and set a plate for the gentleman, Sylvy!" And Sylvia promptly stepped. She was glad to have something to do, and she was hungry herself.

It was a surprise to find so clean and comfortable a little dwelling in this New England wilderness. The young man had known the horrors of its most primitive housekeeping, and the dreary squalor of that level of society which does not rebel at the companionship of hens. This was the best thrift of an old-fashioned farmstead, though on such a small scale that it seemed like a hermitage. He listened eagerly to the old woman's quaint talk, he watched Sylvia's pale face and shining gray eyes with ever growing enthusiasm, and insisted that this was the best supper he had eaten for a month, and afterward the new-made friends sat down in the door-way together while the moon came up.

Generalizations and Conclusions

1. Based on the passage, how does the stranger feel toward Sylvia and her grandmother?

    A. He is suspicious of them.

    B. He feels shy around them.

    C. He enjoys their company.

    D. He wants them to leave him alone.

2. It is clear from the passage that Sylvia is:

    A. an orphaned child.

    B. timid around strange men.

    C. often afraid of her grandmother.

    D. happy to have a visitor.

HUMANITIES: This passage is excerpted from a short contemporary memoir.

    Allie Lawrence was quite bright. I should know, because that's me—the girl with the rosy future, the queen of possibilities. I knew my parents expected a great deal of me, and I was ready to deliver on my promise. I had come out of high school ready to take on the world, but after a few years, my job was nothing more than that—a job. I wanted a career.
5 So I went back to school at night, while I worked during the day. After graduation, I got a position with a company as a computer programmer. It was challenging, and I was good at it. I was promoted within two years and transferred to the corporate headquarters in Chicago. Moving to another state had been difficult. I didn't know anyone, and at twenty-eight, I was just too young to mix socially with my coworkers. All the people in my work
10 group were men in their forties who were already married. But I decided it was no big deal if romance wasn't on my horizon; I was on the fast track, and a relationship would only get in the way of my upward agenda. So I decided to pour myself into my work for a while and try to get promoted and transferred again. I worked hard through another frozen Chicago winter, and yet another simmering city summer—and by the time the leaves
15 turned, so did my luck. A coveted position suddenly came open in the company's booming southern region, and it was mine if I wanted it! The offer was everything I had been dreaming of: a major promotion, an executive title, and a huge raise, along with my very own lavish high-rise office suite in Fort Worth, Texas. It was perfect—almost. There was only one problem. By then, I was in love … and it was my bad timing to have fallen for
20 the one man who so personified Chicago that nothing could tear him away from the city he loved.

Chapter 5

3. Which of the following conclusions can you draw from the passage?

   A. Going to Fort Worth would mean Allie must leave behind the one she loves.

   B. This is the first time that Allie has ever fallen in love.

   C. Allie's boss has told her she cannot take her true love with her to Fort Worth.

   D. Allie feels as if she would gladly give up her career for a chance at true love.

CHAPTER 5 SUMMARY
Below are some key concepts covered in chapter 5 and some reading comprehension skills you need to be prepared to demonstrate on the PLAN Reading Test. **Draw simple generalizations and conclusions about people, ideas, and so on in uncomplicated passages.** **Draw simple generalizations and conclusions about the main characters in uncomplicated literary narratives.** **Draw generalizations and conclusions about people, ideas, and so on in uncomplicated and more challenging passages.** **Draw simple generalizations and conclusions using details that support the main points of more challenging passages.** **Use information from one or more sections of a more challenging passage to draw generalizations and conclusions about people, ideas, and so on.**

Chapter 5 Review

Generalizations and Conclusions

Read the passage below. The questions that follow will allow you to practice the skills covered in this chapter and listed at the beginning of this chapter review.

HUMANITIES: The following is an excerpt from a memoir entitled "Tough Times on the Farm," by Dennis Martin.

I was raised in a small town on the shores of Lake Erie. The big water was only three blocks away from my house, and as a young boy I spent much of my
5 time fishing from its shore with my two friends Sparky and Dave. When I wasn't fishing, I was busy working. Life in the city brought many opportunities for a young boy to make money. First, there
10 was my paper route. I would fold the papers in thirds, tuck in the ends real tight, load them in the basket on the front of my bike, and throw them on the porches of all my customers. Not only
15 did I get paid every week, but during the holiday season I would always receive nice tips from the homeowners. With the changing of the seasons came more means of making money for a boy of
20 industrious inclinations. In the winter, I would shovel the snow off the walks for all the elderly people. In the spring and summer, I would cut their grass, and in the fall I would rake their leaves and
25 clear their lawns of the ubiquitous buckeyes. Life was good and I always had money to spend. But one day my parents said those words that all children hate to hear: "Kids, we're moving."

30 We were renting out our house in the city and moving to the country. The trucks were loaded, and I waved goodbye to my buddies, thinking that I would never see them again. We arrived
35 at our new house in the country on a clear and sunny spring day. The farm house was big and white with a long stone driveway. When I got out of the car to explore the property, I found two large
40 red barns and a chicken coop in need of repair. The wheels in my head starting turning, and I soon struck upon an idea to make money.

"Dad," I said, "I could fix up this
45 chicken coop and buy some chickens." My plan was to set up an egg stand out front by the large oak tree where passersby could stop to get fresh eggs. My father agreed, and in no time I was in
50 the egg business. I bought ten chickens and one bandy rooster, built a small wooden table to set the carton of eggs on, made a sign, and nailed a metal box to the tree where people could insert their
55 money. Every morning I would lift the chickens off their nests and gather up their golden brown treasures. Not only did the money come in at a steady pace, but every morning I enjoyed hearing my
60 young rooster crowing to herald a new day.

There was also plenty of land available for the tilling. I knew there was big money in watermelons and
65 cantaloupes, so I began tilling the soil next to the house. Within a week I had a huge plot of land tilled and planted. I calculated that by the end of summer I would make more money on my melons
70 than the egg business. By the end of July, I could cast my eyes about and see hundreds of melons. With a selling price of a couple dollars per melon, I figured I would soon be as rich as King Midas.

75 All was going well until one stormy night in late July. Lightning and rain pounded the farm all night long.

Chapter 5

Sometime in the middle of the night I thought I heard my chickens raising a fuss. I propped up on one elbow, sleepy and groggy, and strained to hear through the storm, but all I could hear was the clap of lightning and tree branches grinding and slapping into each other. Nothing sounded suspicious, so I fell back to sleep.

There was an eerie calm the next morning as I walked toward the chicken coop. Normally, I would hear purring and cackling, but this morning there was a strange silence. When I opened the door to the coop and entered, I jumped back in horror. Dead chickens lay scattered about on the floor, their throats torn open. I stumbled out the door and ran around to look at the fenced in pen. There too were the rest of my chickens lying dead with my rooster in the middle of them all. I ran up to the house and found my mother in the kitchen. "Something's killed all my chickens!" I screamed.

"What!" she gasped.

"Come and see!" I cried.

She followed me out the door, still clutching a large kitchen towel. "Good God!" she cried when she saw the carnage. My uncle was pulling up the driveway as we went back toward the house. We told him what had happened.

"It was probably a skunk that did it," he said. "They are known to kill chickens and drink their blood."

My uncle and I set about the gruesome business of burying my chickens. One stormy night and one nasty skunk had suddenly, and irrevocably, put me out of the egg business. That night I went to bed and did nothing but blame myself for not getting up the night before to investigate the strange sounds that I had heard. My transition from city boy to country boy had been progressing well until my lack of suspicion and some vicious animal laid me low.

The summer droned on to its inevitable end, and I tried to keep myself busy in my melon patch by weeding and mulching my plants. I still had hundreds of melons to rely on; and I knew that in a few weeks I could turn the egg stand into a melon stand and reap the financial rewards of all my hard work—or so I thought.

In the last week of August I had my tonsils taken out. My parents went into town to buy groceries and left me lounging on the couch sucking on popsicles to soothe my sore throat. I was watching the movie *Moby Dick*, and Captain Ahab was thrusting his harpoon into the great leviathan and cursing him. "Damn you, you cursed whale!" he cried as he fought against that unstoppable force of nature. Suddenly, I heard a loud clap of thunder and looking out the large windows in the dining room I could see bolts of lightning shooting out of the sky and zapping their way down to the ground. The winds grew forceful and intense; the large tree limbs near the house began banging against the roof and gutters. And then I heard it; a most terrible sound—not the sound of rain, but something much more frightful and devastating. The pounding, thumping, and unmistakable sound of HAIL!

"No!" I screamed as I ran to the windows. I stood there in utter terror as I watched millions of white baseball-sized missiles of hail smashing into my melons and turning them into so much

Generalizations and Conclusions

165 fruit salad. Tears streamed down my face; I was devastated and as distraught as one young boy could be. The next day was spent tilling the ruins of my melon patch back into the lush soil and
170 realizing that all my hard work had been for naught and that I would see none of the profits of my labor that I had counted on so dearly.

Fall turned into winter and winter
175 into spring; and just when I was making plans to try my luck again at the farming business, my parents said those words that children hate to hear: "Kids, we're moving." But this time we were
180 returning to our house in the city, and to be honest, I couldn't wait to get back to my old friends and to cast my fishing line into the inviting waters of the big lake.

1. Judging from the passage, which of the following would cause an industrious kid the most anxiety?
   A. Working for money
   B. Moving elsewhere
   C. Growing melons
   D. Having tonsils out

2. From the passage, it is evident that as a child, the narrator liked to:
   F. daydream.
   G. make money.
   H. plan for his future.
   J. spend time with his family.

3. According to the passage, hail is known to:
   A. kill chickens.
   B. ruin trips to the country.
   C. destroy crops.
   D. make people move.

4. Which of the following is most likely an accurate description of the narrator's parents?
   F. They encourage him to work hard and be responsible.
   G. They do not care very much about what he does with his time.
   H. They want him to stay focused mostly on his schoolwork.
   J. They are not supportive of his money-making efforts.

5. Which of the following conclusions is supported by the passage?
   A. The narrator likes growing melons more than running an egg business.
   B. The narrator does not miss his city friends while he lives in the country.
   C. The narrator trusts his uncle's opinion about matters related to the farm.
   D. The narrator has never seen hailstorms before moving to the country.

Chapter 5

6. According to the passage, if a chicken coop is quiet, it is a sure sign that:
    F. a skunk has killed the chickens.
    G. something is wrong.
    H. a hailstorm is coming.
    J. the chickens are laying eggs.

7. Based on the narrator's reaction to the hail, which conclusion can you draw?
    A. The shock of seeing the hailstorm has made him forget the pain in his throat.
    B. Realizing the hailstorm would ruin his crop has made him want his parents.
    C. Knowing that his investment has been ruined has made him feel grown up.
    D. Having a major setback has made him all the more determined to succeed.

8. What element will the narrator probably always associate with plans going wrong?
    F. Classic literature
    G. Fertile soil
    H. Stormy weather
    J. Melon patches

Generalizations and Conclusions

PLAN Reading Test
Practice Test

20 minutes — 25 questions

Directions: There are three passages in this test. Read each of the passages, and then answer the questions that follow. Choose the best answer to each question based on your reading of the passage. You may refer to the passage as often as needed.

Passage I

Directions: Read the passage below. Then answer the questions that follow it. Choose the best answer to each question based on your reading of the passage. You may refer to the passage as often as needed.

SOCIAL SCIENCES: This passage is an essay entitled "Martha: An American Trailblazer" (©2010 American Book Company).

Imagine navigating an unknown world without even a compass to guide you. Martha Washington faced a similar task as our very first First Lady. As wife
5 to America's first president, Martha had no precedent to follow and no clear definition of her role. She was thrust into a position in which she would sink or swim.

10 Martha Dandridge was born on June 2, 1731, in Virginia. She grew up riding horses, dancing, and playing the piano. As was customary, she learned sewing and gardening. However, unlike most
15 girls, Martha also received a formal education in math, reading, and writing.

As a teenager, Martha married Daniel Custis, a man twenty years her senior. Her marriage had the trappings
20 of a fairy tale. They lived in a mansion ironically called the White House. Martha set up housekeeping while her husband ran the plantation and lavished expensive gifts on his bride. However,
25 Martha's story included much unhappiness. The couple had four children, but only two lived past infancy. Then, after a short illness, Daniel died, making Martha a young
30 widow with a three-year-old son, Jacky, and a baby daughter, Patsy.

Two years later, Martha married George Washington. With Martha's substantial inheritance, the family
35 enjoyed a comfortable life on Washington's farm at Mount Vernon. George oversaw the business dealings of the properties, while Martha supervised the household staff, oversaw
40 the harvesting, and accommodated the needs of her household and guests. Martha doted on her children, showering them with attention and gifts. The Washington family continued this
45 lifestyle despite a number of years of poor crop earnings, so their savings dwindled.

Years later, Martha suffered the loss of her daughter, Patsy. At the same time,
50 trouble was brewing in the colonies. Some of the couple's friends began organizing a resistance to oppose England's taxation policies. They urged George to take a leadership position,
55 and George agreed. Martha, however, felt like a rope in a tug-of-war contest. Many of her friends and neighbors, as well as her son's new in-laws, were Loyalists.

60 Despite her trepidations, Martha supported her husband wholly throughout the American Revolution. She traveled great distances to join her husband at army encampments and
65 encouraged other women to support the war effort. When George fell ill, Martha nursed him back to health; and when

Practice Test

other soldiers' families came upon hard times, Martha extended a helping hand
70 despite her own tightening finances.

While war raged, Martha suffered another blow when Jacky died. When his widow became ill, their two youngest children moved in with their
75 grandmother and remained with Martha until adulthood.

After the war, George became the first president of the United States. Martha didn't attend his inauguration.
80 Some historians attribute this to Martha's being delayed by family responsibilities. Others believe her absence, as well as her lack of a public role in his second inauguration, were
85 signs of Martha's unhappiness about her husband's election. Whichever is reality, Martha supported George as he governed the new nation. Having earned the admiration of Americans
90 through her support of the soldiers during the Revolution, Martha earned the respect of the Europeans with her gracious hospitality.

Martha and the grandchildren lived
95 with the president in Philadelphia, the seat of American government at the time, until yellow fever ravaged the city. The family moved back to Mount Vernon until the mosquitoes died off.
100 They returned in the winter, and Martha continued fulfilling her duties to her family and country.

After two presidential terms, the Washingtons retired to Mount Vernon.
105 Shortly after George's death, Martha destroyed all of her correspondence with George except for two letters. In 1802, Martha Dandridge Custis Washington died at Mount Vernon.

1. In lines 8–9 of the passage, what does the phrase "sink or swim" imply?

   A. Martha had to do much research to become the First Lady.
   B. If she did not succeed in her new role, she could always quit.
   C. Due to her demanding position, Martha had no more free time.
   D. Martha could rely on herself and succeed or else give up and fail.

2. Why are historians unable to pinpoint the reason Martha did not attend the inauguration?

   F. She destroyed letters that may have discussed her reasons.
   G. There were no historians or record keepers in the 1700s.
   H. Martha gave different answers to different historians.
   J. The historians were unsure of the laws at that time.

3. Through what means was yellow fever spread throughout Philadelphia?

   A. By mosquito bites
   B. By polluted water
   C. By human touch
   D. By contaminated food

Practice Test

4. In lines 1–3 of the passage, what purpose does the statement "Imagine navigating the world without even a compass to guide you" serve?

    F. It is meant to paint an image of how turbulent Martha's life was.

    G. It serves to illustrate how lost Martha must have felt as First Lady.

    H. It compares the uncertainty she felt in marrying George Washington.

    J. It is imagery meant to show the pain Martha felt losing her children.

5. The passage says that Martha supported her husband George throughout the Revolution "despite her trepidations," which means that she:

    A. wholeheartedly supported the war.

    B. resented having to support her husband.

    C. was indifferent towards the Revolution.

    D. had doubts about the Revolution.

6. Based on the passage, Martha's first husband was a:

    F. cruel taskmaster.

    G. wealthy landowner.

    H. young Englishman.

    J. military leader.

7. Which of the following occurred before the colonies declared independence?

    A. Martha's son Jacky died.

    B. George and Martha lived in Philadelphia.

    C. Martha destroyed all of her letters to George.

    D. The Washington farm yielded poor crop earnings.

8. Martha's attitude toward supporting George best can be described as:

    F. selfless.

    G. bitter.

    H. insecure.

    J. selfish.

Passage II

Directions: Read the passage below. Then answer the questions that follow it. Choose the best answer to each question based on your reading of the passage. You may refer to the passage as often as needed.

PROSE FICTION: This passage is the full text of the short story "John Mortonson's Funeral" by Ambrose Bierce (1906).

John Mortonson was dead: his lines in 'the tragedy "Man"' had all been spoken and he had left the stage.

The body rested in a fine mahogany coffin fitted with a plate of glass. All arrangements for the funeral had been so well attended to that had the deceased known he would doubtless have approved. The face, as it showed under the glass, was not disagreeable to look upon: it bore a faint smile, and as the death had been painless, had not been distorted beyond the repairing power of the undertaker. At two o'clock of the afternoon the friends were to assemble to pay their last tribute of respect to one who had no further need of friends and respect. The surviving members of the family came severally every few minutes to the casket and wept above the placid features beneath the glass. This did them no good; it did no good to John Mortonson; but in the presence of death reason and philosophy are silent.

As the hour of two approached the friends began to arrive and after offering such consolation to the stricken relatives as the proprieties of the occasion required, solemnly seated themselves about the room with an augmented consciousness of their importance in the scheme funereal. Then the minister came, and in that overshadowing presence the lesser lights went into eclipse. His entrance was followed by that of the widow, whose lamentations filled the room. She approached the casket and after leaning her face against the cold glass for a moment was gently led to a seat near her daughter. Mournfully and low the man of God began his eulogy of the dead, and his doleful voice, mingled with the sobbing which it was its purpose to stimulate and sustain, rose and fell, seemed to come and go, like the sound of a sullen sea. The gloomy day grew darker as he spoke; a curtain of cloud underspread the sky and a few drops of rain fell audibly. It seemed as if all nature were weeping for John Mortonson.

When the minister had finished his eulogy with prayer a hymn was sung and the pall-bearers took their places beside the bier. As the last notes of the hymn died away the widow ran to the coffin, cast herself upon it and sobbed hysterically. Gradually, however, she yielded to dissuasion, becoming more composed; and as the minister was in the act of leading her away her eyes sought the face of the dead beneath the glass. She threw up her arms and with a shriek fell backward insensible.

The mourners sprang forward to the coffin, the friends followed, and as the clock on the mantel solemnly struck three all were staring down upon the face of John Mortonson, deceased.

They turned away, sick and faint. One man, trying in his terror to escape the awful sight, stumbled against the coffin so heavily as to knock away one
75 of its frail supports. The coffin fell to the floor, the glass was shattered to bits by the concussion.

From the opening crawled John Mortonson's cat, which lazily leapt to
80 the floor, sat up, tranquilly wiped its crimson muzzle with a forepaw, then walked with dignity from the room.

9. What is the purpose of the first half of the passage?

   A. To describe the church in which the funeral takes place
   B. To give the reader a sense of knowing John Mortonson
   C. To set the mood and scene of the funeral service
   D. To reveal the minister as being insincere

10. This passage can best be summarized as:

    F. people attending a funeral are surprised when they find that the deceased's cat has been shut inside the coffin.
    G. people attending a funeral are surprised to find that the deceased's body is that of another man whom nobody knows.
    H. people attending a funeral are surprised when the deceased's widow demands that they find her another husband.
    J. people attending a funeral are surprised to discover that the weather forecast was for rain and not sunny weather.

11. The author chooses to recount John Mortonson's funeral from the perspective of:

    A. the minister.
    B. the widow.
    C. one of the mourners.
    D. an omniscient narrator.

12. Which of the following can you conclude from the description in the passage?

    F. The funeral is not overly emotional.
    G. John Mortonson's wife deeply loved him.
    H. Someone put a cat in John Mortonson's coffin.
    J. John Mortonson was a charitable man.

Practice Test

13. It is evident that the embalmer who prepares the body for burial:

    A. is new to the profession of undertaking.

    B. has not devoted proper time to preparing the body.

    C. is not familiar with the people attending the funeral.

    D. has been aided by the manner of John Mortonson's death.

14. The author uses the cat to represent the truth that:

    F. pets are very special to their owners.

    G. John Mortonson loved his cat.

    H. life goes on without John Mortonson.

    J. unlike cats, people don't have nine lives.

15. The sight of the dead man's face leads many mourners to:

    A. hurriedly turn away.

    B. think about their own lives.

    C. rush to get a better view.

    D. go to console the widow.

16. According to the passage, the pallbearers take their places beside the bier:

    F. as the minister is praying.

    G. after the widow runs to the coffin.

    H. at approximately two o'clock.

    J. as the congregation finishes a song.

Practice Test

Passage III

Directions: Read the passage below. Then answer the questions that follow it. Choose the best answer to each question based on your reading of the passage. You may refer to the passage as often as needed.

HUMANITIES: This passage is adapted from an essay called "Simplicity" by Charles Dudley Warner (published in 1904 in *The Complete Essays of Charles Dudley Warner*).

I am not sure whether simplicity is a matter of nature or of cultivation. Barbarous nature likes display, excessive ornament; and when we have
5   arrived at the nobly simple, the perfect proportion, we are always likely to relapse into the confused and the complicated. The most cultivated men, we know, are the simplest in manners, in
10 taste, in their style. It is a mark of some of the purest modern writers that they avoid comparisons, similes, and even much use of metaphor. But the mass is always relapsing into the
15 tawdry and the over-ornamented. It is a characteristic of youth, and it seems also to be a characteristic of over-development. Literature, in any language, has no sooner arrived at the
20 highest vigor of simple expression than it begins to run into prettiness, conceits, over-elaboration. This is a fact which may be verified by studying different periods, from classic literature to our
25 own day.

It is the same with architecture. The classic Greek runs into the excessive elaboration of the Roman period, the Gothic into the flamboyant, and so on.
30 We have had several attacks of architectural measles in this country, which have left the land spotted all over with houses in bad taste. Instead of developing the colonial simplicity on
35 lines of dignity and harmony to modern use, we stuck on the pseudo-classic, we broke out in the Mansard, we broke all up into the whimsicalities of the so-called Queen Anne, without regard to
40 climate or comfort. The eye speedily tires of all these things. It is a positive relief to look at an old colonial mansion, even if it is as plain as a barn. What the eye demands is simple lines, proportion, harmony in mass, dignity; above all, adaptation to use. And what we must have also is individuality in house and in furniture; the country, the city, the village, picturesque and interesting. The
50 highest thing in architecture, as in literature, is the development of individuality in simplicity.

[…] Simplicity is not ugliness, nor poverty, nor barrenness, nor necessarily
55 plainness. What is simplicity for another may not be for you, for your needs are different, especially for your wants. It is a serious question. […]

60 The needs of every person differ from the needs of every other; we can make no standard for wants or possessions. But the world would be greatly transformed and much more
65 easy to live in if everybody limited his acquisitions to his ability to assimilate them to his life. The destruction of simplicity is a craving for things, not because we need them, but because
70 others have them. Because one man

108

who lives in a plain little house, in all the restrictions of mean surroundings, would be happier in a mansion suited to his taste and his wants, is no argument
75 that another man, living in a palace, in useless ostentation, would not be better off in a dwelling which conforms to his cultivation and habits. It is so hard to learn the lesson that there is no
80 satisfaction in gaining more than we personally want.

The matter of simplicity, then, comes into literary style, into building, into dress, into life, individualized
85 always by one's personality. In each we aim at the expression of the best that is in us, not at imitation or ostentation.

17. According to the passage, humankind's desire for more possessions:

    A. has made life harder to bear.
    B. encourages individuality and simplicity.
    C. leads to harmony among the people.
    D. leaves the land spotted with houses.

18. Which of the following would the author consider a characteristic of a cultivated man?

    F. Appreciating modern architecture
    G. Being able to acquire many possessions
    H. Possessing the ability to speak well
    J. Exhibiting simple tastes and manners

19. In lines 3–4 of the passage, the phrase "Barbarous nature likes display, excessive ornament" means that the author holds what belief?

    A. Most people lack the ability to become cultivated.
    B. Wealthy people cannot learn to appreciate simplicity.
    C. Unrefined people have a tendency to overdo things.
    D. Refined people desire exciting and rich surroundings.

20. According to the author, in what way are literature and architecture similar?

    F. They are both excessive and overly ornate.
    G. They both are best when they are kept simple.
    H. The classic styles of both have given way to modernity.
    J. They both should resist the use of similes and metaphors.

21. What quality can the reader conclude that the author values?

    A. Intellect
    B. Creativity
    C. Practicality
    D. Cautiousness

Practice Test

22. According to the passage, the author's reference to a colonial mansion is meant to serve what purpose?

F. As an example of the overcomplicated

G. As evidence supporting the author's argument

H. As evidence of Americans' lack of simplicity

J. As a metaphor for people's acquisition of things

23. According to the passage, which of the following fights against simplicity?

A. Indifference

B. Bitterness

C. Maturity

D. Greed

24. According to the passage, simplicity in literature:

F. cannot be sustained.

G. has never been attained.

H. has been forever lost.

J. has finally been reached.

25. Which of the following ideas does the author reject?

A. Ornamentation is necessary for beauty and intrigue.

B. Simplicity is denied by the desire for possessions.

C. Most men naturally choose the elaborate over the simple.

D. Literature and architecture can both achieve simplicity.

A
allegory 67
allusion 67
analogy 67
author
   purpose 42
author's approach 40
author's point of view 40

B
basic facts 31

C
cause-effect transitions 56
cause-effect relationships 57
chronological order 52
clear intent of the author 41
compare and contrast transitions 55
comparison 55, 73
conclusion 37
context 72
context clue 73
contrast 55, 73

D
definition or restatement 73
descriptive language 66
details
   to support a point in passage 33
draw conclusions 87

E
effect 56
events 32
example 32, 73

F
figurative language 67, 68, 72
first-person point of view 41

G
generalization 81
genre 40

H
hyperbole 67

I
imagery 67
implication 28
implied main idea 28
inference 28
introduction 37
irony
   dramatic 68
   situational 68
   verbal 68

L
limited point of view 41

M
main idea 26

metaphor 68

N
nonfigurative words 72

O
omniscient point of view 41
onomatopoeia 68
organizational pattern 52

P
personification 68
point of view
   types of 41
purpose 26

R
relationships
   people, ideas, and events 55

S
second-person point of view 41
sequence of events 52
signal word 73
simile 68
supporting details 31, 37
symbolism 68

T
third-person point of view 41
time order 52
tips
   finding stated main idea 28
   locating details 31
topic sentence 37
transition 52, 56
transitional element 37

U
understand the dynamics
   people, ideas, and events 55